Currents of Being

Volume II: Eternal Wisdom

SHAHIN SAMADI

Dedication

To my beloved family—those remarkable souls who came before me, whose resilience and wisdom laid the groundwork for all that we are, and to those who will carry forward our legacy, lighting the path into the future with their own dreams and stories. This book is a tribute to each of you, woven from the threads of our shared history and boundless love.

Acknowledgment

I extend my deepest gratitude to my mother, the most senior member of our family, whose unwavering support and rich reservoir of knowledge have been indispensable to this project. Her patience and readiness to address my endless queries have profoundly shaped this endeavor.

The creation of this manuscript involved rigorous research, utilizing an array of resources that spanned online databases such as Wikipedia and Encyclopedia Iranica, alongside numerous books in both English and Persian. Special thanks to online resources like Google and OpenAI's ChatGPT-4, whose capabilities were invaluable for sourcing, fact-checking, and refining content, greatly enhancing its accuracy and clarity.

This thorough exploration was pivotal in ensuring the authenticity and factual integrity of these pages' narratives and historical contexts. While this book is a personal memoir rather than a scholarly text, the depth of the resources consulted was considerable. Though a formal bibliography is omitted, my appreciation for the extensive materials available to me, which significantly enriched and validated the narrative, is immense.

My heartfelt thanks go to everyone who contributed to the creation of this book, whether directly or indirectly, through the wealth of resources that guided and informed my writing journey.

Table of Contents

General Introduction

"Life is no brief candle to me. It is a sort of splendid torch which I have got hold of for the moment, and I want to make it burn as brightly as possible before handing it on to future generations." -
George Bernard Shaw

Time sweeps us forward relentlessly, and our lives whirl along with it. When I pause to reflect, thousands of memories dance before my eyes—moments so vivid and significant they promise to linger until my final breath. These are the memories that color our existence, weaving through the fabric of our days, forever a part of us. One such memory that stands out for me with the vividness of a cherished masterpiece—a serene family picnic on the banks of a picturesque river in Iran from my childhood. This family picnic is forever etched in the depths of my memory. It was a moment of tranquility, framed by the gentle flow of the river, where my father and I sat together, deeply immersed in the beauty of our surroundings. This peaceful scene, captured in my mind like a precious painting, remains a cherished symbol of connection and serenity.

With profound wisdom as timeless as the river, my father turned to me and spoke words that would echo in my mind through the years: "Shahin, observe the continual currents of the water. Life will propel you forward just as swiftly."

When I heard his words, I could not comprehend the depth of his analogy. But with the passage of time, I began to understand the truth behind his words.

With each relationship I formed, every place I explored, each educational institution I joined, and every professional role I assumed, I have realized that these experiences are integral to the winding path of my destiny. My life is like a river, coursing through diverse landscapes, shaping my "Current of Being," which mirrors the concept of the river of life. This metaphor vividly captures how my existence flowed forward, shaped by the choices and interactions I encountered, much like how a river is sculpted by the terrain it flows through. Upholding the tranquility and purposefulness of this flow has been my sacred duty as I gently navigate through the varied terrains of my existence. This analogy enriches my understanding of life's journey, emphasizing the continuous and dynamic nature of personal growth and transformation.

I believe this calmness provides a precious opportunity to appreciate the beauty that resides both within us and in the world around us. Life moves relentlessly, sweeping us through its currents of experiences, challenges, and opportunities, sometimes with dizzying speed. Yet, within the rush of life's river lies a beauty that exceeds its hurried pace—a beauty that leaves an ineffaceable mark upon our souls with each passing moment.

At times, it becomes clear that we must rise as skilled navigators of our own lives, steering our course with grace and wisdom. As we guide our journey through peaceful waters, each moment and experience unfolds into a cherished jewel, enhancing the richness of our path. By mastering the art of navigation, we ensure that our lives are not merely lived but beautifully crafted into a tapestry of memorable moments.

And just as the river flows onward, we, too, must embrace the flow of life, routing its twists and turns with courage and flexibility. My father's words remind me to embrace my journey as the river of life, flow with the rhythm of life, and find comfort in knowing that, no matter how swiftly the current may carry us, we are never alone in our journey.

As we navigate the winding river of life, we often find ourselves adrift, reaching shores far from where our roots first took hold. It is vital, in these moments, to consciously preserve the connections to our ancestors. These ties not only anchor us but also shape our journey, infusing our lives with meaning and direction. By honoring where we come from, we navigate the future with a deeper sense of purpose and understanding.

Maintaining a sense of continuity with our past is essential as we course into the future. By cherishing and safeguarding our memories, we ensure that the essence of our origins is preserved in the currents of change and progress. This mindful preservation of our roots provides a grounding force, a compass that guides us through life's meandering paths while enriching our journey with a deep sense of identity and belonging.

I have divided my book into two parts. Volume I, "The River of Life," is a memoir driven by my deep-seated desire to preserve my journey and honor my heritage. It ensures that the legacy of my ancestors remains vivid and accessible to future generations, especially my children and their descendants. This part of the book recounts my life story and offers detailed descriptions of Iran, appealing to readers interested in understanding the country's rich cultural and historical events.

It serves as a bridge spanning across time, connecting the rich culture of our past with the unfolding chapters of our future. More than a mere retelling of my personal experiences, this part is dedicated to weaving together the threads of history, tradition, and familial bonds, painting a portrait of the journey that has shaped not just me but my entire lineage.

Volume I chronicles my journey and the formation of my perspectives, setting the foundation for the insights explored in Volume II.

In Volume II, "Eternal Wisdom," I delve into the essence of

genuine wisdom, which involves recognizing the interconnectedness of our actions and their effects on individuals and the world. This section emphasizes the importance of lifelong learning and adaptation, drawing on my diverse experiences to deepen our understanding of life's complexities.

From my experiences, I have learned that as we venture into the future, guided by scientific exploration and technological advancement, we discover insights into humanity's potential and the importance of resilience and continual growth. With these reflections, I span diverse topics, from religion and science to technology and human relationships, each shaped by personal experiences, historical insights, and philosophical inquiry. My reflections invite you on a journey of exploration, challenging beliefs, and celebrating the diverse ways we seek understanding in our world.

The eloquent teachings of Persian poets Rumi, Saadi, and Omar Khayyam poignantly remind us that knowledge and perception are inherently relative. Their poetry sheds light on the complexities of human understanding and urges us to embrace a spectrum of perspectives. Their approach deepens our understanding and helps us appreciate the nuanced and multifaceted nature of truth.

"Elephant in the Dark" is a poem by Jalal ad-Din

Muhammad Rumi. A revered 13th-century Persian poet, theologian, and Sufi mystic, Rumi masterfully illustrates the tale of a group of men who, in a dark room, touch different parts of an elephant, each perceiving it differently based on the part they touch. This narrative, originating from a Buddhist parable, highlights the theme of subjective experience and the limitations of perception.

"Some Hindus have an elephant to display.
No one here has ever seen an elephant.
They bring it at night to a dark room.
One by one, we go in the dark and come out
saying how we experience the animal.
One of us happens to touch the trunk.
A water-pipe kind of creature.
Another, the ear. A very strong, always moving
back and forth, fan-animal. Another, the leg.
I find it still, like a column on a temple.
Another touches the curved back.
A leathery throne. Another the cleverest,
feels the tusk. A rounded sword made of porcelain.
He is proud of his description.
Each of us touches one place
and understands the whole that way.
The palm and the fingers feeling in the dark
are how the senses explore the reality of the elephant.

If each of us held a candle there,

and if we went in together, we could see it."

In Rumi's depiction, several people present an elephant in a pitch-dark room. The visitors, feeling different parts of the elephant, come away with distinct interpretations of the creature. One encounters the trunk and thinks it resembles a water pipe; another feels the ear and concludes it is like a fan; yet another touches the leg and likens it to a temple's column. The diverse descriptions stem from their limited interactions, leading each to a unique, albeit partial, understanding of the elephant.

Rumi uses this story to emphasize the relativity of truth and the importance of seeing the whole before making judgments. This parable urges an openness to multiple perspectives and a recognition of our own subjective limitations. His teachings have crossed national and ethnic boundaries, resonating through the centuries with universal insights into love, humanity, and the pursuit of truth. Rumi's work, celebrated for its profound expression and deep spirituality, has been translated into numerous languages and continues to inspire a global audience.

Complementing Rumi's reflections on the nature of perception and truth, the famous Persian poem by Sheikh Saadi Shirazi, another esteemed Persian poet and philosopher from the medieval period, explores themes of self-awareness and wisdom:

"If you know and you know that you know,
You are wise, follow him.
If you know not, and you know that you know not,
You are simple, teach him.
If you know, yet you know not that you know,
You are asleep, awaken him.
If you know not, and you know not that you know not,
You are a fool, shun him."

Saadi's verses articulate the importance of recognizing one's level of knowledge and adapting one's interactions based on this awareness. These lines offer guidance on how to approach learning and interaction—whether to lead, teach, awaken, or avoid—based on the degree of awareness and ignorance. This poem reflects knowledge, ignorance, and how we engage with others, providing timeless wisdom on navigating the complexities of human understanding and relationships.

As I reflect on the nature of knowledge and the passage of time, Omar Khayyam's words resonate with me deeply:

"With them the Seed of Wisdom did I sow,
And with my own hand labour'd it to grow:
And this was all the Harvest that I reap'd—
"I came like Water, and like Wind I go."

These lines capture the essence of our human experience—

our ceaseless striving to cultivate wisdom, only to realize that our time on earth is as transient as water flowing or the wind blowing. This introduction sets the stage for exploring how the pursuit of knowledge shapes our lives, the legacies we aim to leave behind, and the ultimate recognition of life's fleeting nature. As we delve into the themes of this discussion, let us consider how wisdom influences our journey, even as we move inexorably toward the end of our time.

While I do not profess to offer definitive answers to the topics addressed within these pages, what unfolds in each section is far more than mere personal opinion; it is a synthesis of my lifelong learnings, keen observations, and thoughtful reflections. This book is crafted to resonate on a deeper intellectual and emotional level and invites you, the reader, to engage with these insights. Viewing them through the prism of your experiences may challenge or reinforce your beliefs. This is an invitation to a dialogue between my reflections and your perspectives, fostering a richer understanding of the subjects discussed.

Therefore, I welcome you to a journey that traverses the intricate mosaic of human experience, exploring the diverse ways we perceive and engage with our world. As you turn these pages, you are invited to delve into the complexities of perception and the inherently subjective nature of understanding. Through engaging with these themes, we seek to grasp the expansive spectrum of human thought and recognize the subtle nuances that shape both our personal and collective realities within the ever-flowing "Currents of Being." This book is an invitation to reflect, challenge, and deepen our understanding of the richly varied human narrative.

Volume Two Introduction

"Small minds talk about people, average minds talk about events, great minds talk about ideas" - Eleanor Roosevelt

My passion for learning has been a cornerstone of my personal and professional development since early childhood. This love for knowledge continues into my adulthood, where I set a personal goal to read—or listen to—at least one non-technical book each month. Staying updated in a rapidly advancing technological field necessitates delving into technical books and journal papers that enhance my expertise. However, my interests extend beyond technology as I explore various topics that pique my curiosity.

Reading has always been a gateway to both knowledge and relaxation. Books provided adventure and learning during my childhood, fueling my imagination and expanding my horizons. This early habit laid a strong foundation for my later educational and professional pursuits. In the fast-paced world of technology, staying abreast of the latest trends and innovations is essential. Reading the technical and business literature informs me about new advancements, methodologies, and best practices, ensuring my skills and knowledge remain cutting-edge.

Beyond my professional sphere, my reading interests are

diverse. I enjoy biographies, history, psychology, economics, and other areas of nonfiction that offer insights into various aspects of life and the human experience. This broader reading habit allows me to gain a well-rounded perspective, enriching my understanding of the world and contributing to personal growth.

For instance, biographies provide deep dives into the lives of influential individuals, offering lessons in resilience, leadership, and creativity. History books help me understand the complex events and decisions that have shaped our current world, providing context for contemporary issues. Psychology books explore the workings of the human mind, enhancing my understanding of behavior, motivation, and interpersonal relationships. Similarly, books on economics offer valuable insights into the forces that drive markets, influence policy, and affect global prosperity.

Listening to audiobooks has become a convenient way to keep up with my reading goals despite a busy schedule. Audiobooks provide a flexible means to explore various subjects, whether commuting, exercising, walking my dog, or relaxing at home.

My lifelong love for reading keeps me informed, inspired, and connected to various ideas and knowledge, fueling my curiosity and passion for learning. The benefits of reading are manifold and not restricted to professional growth. Diving into books from various fields fuels my creativity, broadening my perspective and fostering a deeper understanding of the world. Moreover, reading serves as a powerful stress-relief tool. It offers a respite from the daily grind, allowing me to immerse myself in other worlds and ideas. This rejuvenates my mind and enhances my well-being, providing a balanced approach to handling the pressures of life and work.

The inspiration drawn from the lives and insights of others motivates me to pursue new ambitions and apply innovative strategies personally and professionally. Exposure to diverse perspectives enriches my problem-solving approach and enhances my social interactions.

Engaging with various topics also helps me connect with different people and foster meaningful conversations. Whether discussing historical events, economic theories, or psychological insights, my varied reading interests provide common ground for engaging and insightful dialogues with individuals from various backgrounds.

Reading books provides knowledge, expands your understanding, and introduces you to new ideas and concepts. However, true wisdom comes from life experience. While books can open your mind to new perspectives, experiencing life firsthand—facing challenges, making decisions, and observing the outcomes—is knowledge transformed into wisdom. When you live through events, witness real-life situations, and encounter various people, you see the practical application of your acquired knowledge. This experiential learning allows you to internalize lessons deeply, leading to a profound and nuanced understanding of the world. In essence, books plant the seeds of knowledge, but life experience nurtures these seeds into the rich, insightful harvest of wisdom.

This part of my book begins by inviting readers into a reflective journey through the rich and varied landscapes of human experience. It recognizes that wisdom is not a destination but a journey continually shaped and enriched by our daily experiences. It posits that each moment holds learning potential, and every experience, be it joyous or challenging, contributes a unique strand to this tapestry.

The narrative delves into how wisdom is often born from the crucible of our trials and triumphs, shaped by the decisions we make and the obstacles we overcome. It suggests that wisdom is not solely acquired through formal education but is also gleaned from the quiet reflections of a solitary walk, the empathy gleaned from comforting a friend, or the insights gained in overcoming personal adversity.

Furthermore, "Eternal Wisdom" explores the concept that true wisdom involves understanding the interconnectedness of our actions and their impact on others and the world around us. It champions the idea that lifelong learning is a continuous process of adapting, growing, and understanding oneself and the larger tapestry of life.

As we navigate towards the uncharted realms of tomorrow, we embark with minds receptive to new ideas and steadfast determination. Within the dynamic arena of scientific exploration, we uncover the blueprints for our future and a deeper understanding of our very humanity. Each discovery is a stepping stone, teaching us resilience, adaptability, and the relentless pursuit of knowledge. These are the lessons that don't just propel us forward scientifically but also enrich our collective human experience, reminding us of our endless potential for growth and understanding.

Throughout my life's journey, as detailed in the first volume, "The River of Life," I have traversed diverse terrains of experiences and understanding, forming my opinions on a wide array of topics. These range from profound and philosophical subjects, such as religion, to the practical and ever-evolving fields of science and technology. I have also delved into the intricate dynamics of human relationships and other areas that touch upon the essence of our existence and advancement as a society. I intend to share these reflections in the following sections, offering a window into my perspective on these pivotal domains.

Human relationships, a cornerstone of our existence, are a complex web of emotions, social norms, and psychological underpinnings. My views here are colored by my experiences and observations, encompassing the various ways we interact, communicate, and connect with one another.

In the sphere of science, my opinions are informed by the relentless pursuit of knowledge and an appreciation for the empirical method that underpins scientific inquiry. Science, for me, is not just a collection of facts but a dynamic process of understanding the world.

Technology, a byproduct of scientific advancement, is another area of deep interest for me. My perspective on technology encompasses its incredible potential to transform lives, the ethical dilemmas it presents, and its role in shaping our future.

Regarding religion, my views have been shaped by a blend of personal experiences, historical understanding, and philosophical inquiry. This is a realm where faith meets tradition, and personal belief intersects with communities' collective consciousness.

Each of the following sections is more than just an exposition of opinions; it is a distillation of my life's learnings, observations, and reflections. It invites the reader to explore these realms from a personal perspective, possibly challenging their beliefs or reinforcing them. This journey through my thoughts is an exploration of the diversity of human experience and an acknowledgment of the myriad ways we seek to understand our world and our place within it.

Connections and Crossroads: The Journey of Human Relationships

"In the hopes of reaching the moon, men fail to see the flowers that blossom at their feet."— Albert Schweitzer

The 14th-century Arab historian and sociologist Ibn Khaldun, in his seminal work "Muqaddimah," laid the groundwork for various fields of study, including historiography, sociology, economics, and the philosophy of history. "Muqaddimah," also known as "The Introduction," is regarded as one of the earliest works to systematically analyze the social, economic, and political dynamics that influence the rise and fall of civilizations. Independently, the 18th-century Scottish historian Adam Ferguson, in his work "An Essay on the History of Civil Society," posits that the stages of a dynasty are barbarism, civilization, and decadence. Each stage represents a phase in the natural life cycle of human societies, reflecting a shared understanding across different eras and cultures about the development and decline of civilizations.

This observation suggests that civilizations inherently progress through a predictable sequence of development. They emerge from a state of barbarism, establish themselves in a phase of civilization, and then, with prosperity, enter a period of decadence.

However, Ibn Khaldun warns that with prosperity comes complacency and moral decay, leading to a period of decadence where societal structures weaken and civilization ultimately declines. This cyclical view implies that no society is immune to the forces of change and decay. It underscores the importance of vigilance and renewal, as these are the keys to sustaining a civilization's vitality in the face of inevitable change.

The evolution of social interactions as societies progress from barbarism to civilization and eventually to decadence reflects significant changes in how people relate to one another. In the initial stage of barbarism, interactions are primarily focused on survival. Communities are tight-knit, based on kinship or tribal affiliations, with strong loyalty and solidarity among members. Conflict and warfare with other groups are common, as interactions are often marked by competition for resources and territory. As societies progress to civilization, interactions become more complex and structured. Establishing organized institutions, such as governments and legal systems, regulates behavior and maintains order. Cultural advancements and economic systems foster interactions that are more sophisticated and enriched. However, the influence and power of societal norms and values are also evident, as civilized societies often impose their norms and values on others, sometimes through colonization or cultural dominance.

In the stage of decadence, social interactions undergo a

significant transformation. The initial unity and structure of civilization give way to complacency and moral decay. There is a noticeable decline in the enforcement and adherence to established norms and values. Interactions become characterized by a growing tolerance for diverse behaviors and lifestyles, often leading to a lack of social cohesion. The once rigid social structures become more permissive, allowing for a greater degree of individualism and contributing to a fragmentation of the communal bonds that once held society together. This phase of decadence, with its potential for both innovation and decline, reflects a shift from structured and sophisticated relations to more permissive and fragmented interactions, underscoring the complexity and fragility of societal cohesion.

Contemporary scholars have both endorsed and criticized these cyclical theories. Some assert that they offer a valuable framework for interpreting historical trends and emphasizing the roles of social cohesion and leadership. However, others argue that these models may oversimplify complex socio-political dynamics and fail to account for the unique factors shaping each civilization's trajectory. Therefore, I present my perspective on this issue.

As individuals, we must learn to transform our social interactions towards genuine vitality to avoid decadence. While decadence promotes unchecked permissiveness and moral decay, true vitality fosters a stable and cohesive society. In a "stage of vitality," social interactions emphasize inclusivity and respect for diversity in a balanced manner. There is a recognition and appreciation of various cultures, beliefs, and lifestyles within society, but without abandoning core values and social cohesion. Interactions are guided by a strong emphasis on individual rights and freedoms, such as freedom of speech, religion, and expression, while maintaining a commitment to shared societal norms and values. This approach nurtures societal vitality, ensuring a dynamic, thriving community where diversity and core values coexist harmoniously.

Reducing discrimination and promoting equality are essential for fostering more equitable social interactions. Encouraging intercultural dialogue helps to build mutual understanding and respect among different cultural groups, which is crucial for a cohesive society. As social norms become more flexible and adaptive, they allow for innovation and change while preserving social cohesion. This progression reflects a shift from survival-based interactions to more structured and sophisticated relations and, finally, to inclusive and vibrant engagements that value diversity and individual freedoms. By balancing inclusivity and adherence to core values, society can ensure its vitality and resilience, preventing the decline associated with decadence. This balanced approach nurtures a dynamic and thriving community where diversity and core values coexist harmoniously, supporting the overall health and stability of the society.

My Parents' wisdom on humility and respect has been a guiding beacon throughout my life. Their words, "You may not feel the need to look up to anyone, but be certain never to look down on anyone," resonate deeply with me, encapsulating a profound philosophy of equality and empathy. This advice is more than a lesson in humility; it's a fundamental principle for navigating the complexities of human relationships and understanding the inherent value in every person we encounter.

But their wisdom didn't stop there. They often added, "Put yourself in that person's shoes. Would you have fared any better given their circumstances?" This aspect of their advice has been equally transformative, teaching me the power of empathy and perspective-taking. It's a reminder to consider the myriad factors that shape a person's life—factors often beyond their control, like their upbringing, environment, and the unique challenges they've faced.

This guidance is more than just a call for humility; it's an invitation to acknowledge the inherent value in every person we encounter. It's a reminder that while admiration for others can be optional, respect is fundamental. By not looking down on anyone, we recognize the shared humanity that binds us all, embracing an ethos of empathy and understanding.

My parent's words encourage a balanced view of the world,

where we don't measure our worth against others but appreciate each individual's unique contribution to life. This philosophy has shaped my interactions, teaching me to approach relationships with a sense of equality and mutual respect. It's a principle that can transform personal connections and the wider community, fostering an environment of inclusivity and acceptance.

In the mosaic of my life's journey, I've encountered individuals from diverse races, backgrounds, religions, and nationalities. This rich tapestry of human interactions has revealed a fundamental truth about our shared humanity: irrespective of our differences, we all have a universal yearning for love and appreciation. This hunger for emotional connection and recognition transcends all our superficial divides, uniting us in our most basic human needs.

In our modern society, the principle of "live and let live" is often overshadowed by the tendency of established civilizations and individualistic cultures to enforce their beliefs and opinions on others without truly understanding them. This enforcement, whether from organized societal structures or the rise of individualism, can create tensions and conflict, disrupting the delicate balance of coexistence.

Civilized societies or 'civilized individuals' throughout history have often imposed their ideologies and practices on others, sometimes intending to civilize what they deemed as less advanced cultures. This imposition was rooted in a belief that their way of life was superior and that others would benefit from adopting their practices and beliefs. However, such actions frequently led to resistance, cultural erosion, and a lack of mutual respect and understanding. For instance, during the colonial era, European powers imposed their cultural, religious, and social norms on colonized peoples, often disregarding and undermining indigenous traditions and beliefs.

On the other hand, the rise of individualism in contemporary society brings its own set of challenges. While individualism champions personal freedom and self-expression, it can also lead to ideological enforcement, where individuals or groups insist that their way of living or thinking is the only valid one. This insistence can be just as oppressive as the enforced conformity of civilizations, leading to societal decadence and fragmentation. The tendency to prioritize personal beliefs over communal harmony can create divisions and a lack of cohesion within society.

Despite these challenges, living in a structured society while maintaining our individual beliefs without imposing them on others is possible. The key lies in fostering a culture of mutual respect and understanding. By embracing the principle of "live and let live," we acknowledge the diversity of thought, belief, and practice as a strength rather than a threat. This approach allows for a harmonious coexistence where structured societal norms coexist with individual freedoms.

A structured society can provide the necessary framework for order and stability while allowing space for individual expression and diversity. This balance can be achieved through dialogue, empathy, and the willingness to understand and appreciate different perspectives. For example, democratic societies often balance individual rights with collective responsibilities, creating laws and institutions that protect personal freedoms while promoting the common good.

The "live and let live" principle offers a path to a more inclusive and harmonious society. By recognizing and respecting the diversity of beliefs and practices, we can build a community that values structure and individualism. This balance is essential for fostering a society where everyone can coexist peacefully, maintaining their beliefs without imposing them on others. This approach enhances social cohesion and enriches our communities' cultural fabric, ensuring societal vitality.

Achieving a vitality stage in societal development means embracing diversity and inclusivity as core values while maintaining the necessary societal stability frameworks. By fostering a culture of mutual respect and understanding, we can create an environment where "live and let live" is not just a principle but a practice that encourages individual growth and collective harmony. This balanced approach nurtures a dynamic and thriving community, supporting society's overall health and resilience.

As we each have unique physical characteristics, our emotions are fundamental components of the human experience, shaped by biological predispositions and environmental influences. From basic survival instincts like fear to more complex feelings such as joy and sadness, emotions play vital roles in social interactions and personal well-being. Additionally, our emotional landscape is shaped by cultural and societal norms, which influence how we express and manage our feelings. Crucially, emotions such as empathy and sympathy are indispensable for nurturing relationships and enabling effective social interactions. These interactions are essential for our mental and emotional health, providing support systems that enhance our resilience and overall quality of life. Social connections help reduce stress, increase happiness, and foster a sense of belonging, underscoring the importance of emotional bonds in human society.

Samira, my wife, possesses an exceptional degree of emotional intelligence and empathy, qualities that naturally draw people towards her. Her sincere care and attentive listening create a space where people feel genuinely heard and understood. Being in her company has been an enlightening experience for me, especially in human relationships.

Through Samira, I've observed that life is an expansive journey of continuous learning and personal growth. Her interactions remind me that everyone, regardless of background, has a unique story and wisdom. This insight has profoundly influenced my perspective, fostering a deep sense of humility within me.

I've come to appreciate that knowledge and wisdom are not the exclusive domains of a privileged few. Instead, they are abundantly distributed across the diverse canvas of human experiences. Every encounter offers a potential learning opportunity, and every person I meet could be a teacher in their own right if only I am open to the lessons they offer.

Living with Samira and observing her interactions has reinforced the idea that the complexities of human relationships are fertile ground for personal development and understanding. It's an odyssey that requires listening, understanding, and truly appreciating —a journey enriched by every conversation, shared story, and empathetic connection. Samira's approach to life and relationships has been a powerful lesson in embracing the diversity of human experience as an invaluable source of learning and enrichment.

Approaching life with humility has profoundly enriched my understanding and appreciation of the world. It's about recognizing that everyone, from the schoolteacher and the street vendor to the corporate executive and the stay-at-home parent, possesses unique insights and perspectives that can deepen our understanding of life and relationships.

This journey has illuminated for me the invaluable lessons that can be gleaned from every interaction. Each encounter presents an opportunity to learn, grow, and expand our comprehension of the complex and beautiful human experience. Embracing this mindset requires an open heart and mind, acknowledging that the teacher can be anyone and the classroom can be anywhere.

This humble approach to life and relationships continually reshapes and refines my perspective, reminding me of our shared human journey's endless possibilities for growth and connection. It underscores the importance of listening, learning, and engaging with others, fostering a richer, more empathetic understanding of the world around us.

Throughout life, we encounter a myriad of lessons, some uplifting and others challenging. It's essential to recognize that we as individuals are shaped by a complex interplay of nature and nurture, which molds our behaviors and attitudes. This realization brings an understanding that not all interactions will be positive despite our best intentions and actions.

In navigating this journey, we may encounter those whose actions and reactions are puzzling or hurtful. Despite extending kindness and goodwill, we might find ourselves on the receiving end of hostility or malice. This can be a difficult lesson that teaches us about the varied facets of human behavior.

Such experiences remind us that while we can control our actions and responses, we cannot always anticipate or influence how others act toward us. This does not necessarily reflect our behavior or character but often manifests the other individual's personal experiences, perceptions, and emotional state.

While challenging, these encounters provide valuable insights instrumental to our personal growth. They teach us essential life skills such as setting boundaries, practicing resilience, and cultivating empathy for those grappling with their internal struggles. These experiences also underscore the importance of understanding and forgiveness—not only towards others but also towards ourselves—as we navigate the complexities of human relationships.

Exposure to diverse situations and people enriches us with empathy and knowledge, laying the foundation for genuine appreciation, humility, and confidence. Conversely, ignorance poses a significant risk by fostering misconceptions and arrogance, leading us away from the truth and understanding that underpin meaningful interactions and personal development. Prejudice and discrimination are often born out of this ignorance, creating barriers that hinder our ability to connect with and learn from others.

When we allow prejudice to influence our judgments and actions, we miss the richness of different perspectives. Discrimination harms those targeted and impoverishes our lives by limiting our experiences and understanding. Embracing diversity and challenging experiences helps us build a more compassionate and informed worldview, which is essential for fostering healthy relationships and personal growth.

We foster an environment where empathy and respect thrive by actively challenging our biases and engaging with various people and experiences. This commitment to openness and learning helps us to see beyond superficial differences, recognizing the shared humanity that binds us all. Doing so builds meaningful connections and contributes to a more just and equitable society.

It's crucial, however, to distinguish between learning from these interactions and accepting negative behavior. Recognizing that not all lessons are positive is essential to personal growth and emotional intelligence. It guides us to approach relationships with an open heart and a discerning mind, seeking to learn from each experience while prioritizing our well-being and self-respect.

In guiding my sons through the nuances of interpersonal relationships, Samira and I often use the mirror analogy to illustrate how our emotions and attitudes can be reflected in our interactions with others. I explain to them that when we engage with people, the emotional state we bring to the conversation often acts like a reflection in a mirror. The energy and feelings we project have the potential to be mirrored back to us by the person we're interacting with.

For instance, if we approach someone with a visibly upset demeanor, the other person is likely to respond with similar negative emotions, such as defensiveness or discomfort. On the other hand, if we engage with happiness, positivity, or empathy, we're more likely to elicit a corresponding reaction of warmth, openness, and understanding. This reciprocal nature of emotional exchange is fundamental in human communication.

We emphasize to our sons the importance of being mindful of their own emotional states when interacting with others. By recognizing and managing their emotions, they can positively influence the tone of their interactions. It's about understanding that while we can't control how others feel or behave, we can certainly influence it through our own behavior.

This lesson extends beyond mere mimicry of emotions; it's about the more profound principles of empathy and emotional intelligence. It teaches them to be aware of their feelings and those of others and how these emotions can shape the dynamics of a conversation or relationship.

By grasping the concept of emotional reflection, they learn

the value of approaching interactions with intentionality and awareness, cultivating positive relationships, and understanding the power they hold in shaping their social environment.

I've encountered individuals harboring prejudices and stereotypes toward me and others throughout my life. These experiences have taught me a valuable lesson about the roots of such biases. I've come to understand that stereotyping often stems from a need for more exposure and interaction with diverse groups of people. It's a problem rooted in unfamiliarity and a narrow world understanding.

An example of this can be seen in the aftermath of the US hostage crisis in Iran in 1979. During this period, all Iranians were stereotyped, and there were various prejudices against them, even though most Iranians living in the United States did not support the government that took over Iran. This broad-brush approach led to widespread discrimination and negative assumptions about Iranian people, irrespective of their individual beliefs or political stances. Many Iranians in America faced hostility, suspicion, and alienation simply because of their national origin.

A more recent example of this phenomenon occurred during the COVID-19 pandemic. People of Asian descent, particularly those who looked Chinese, faced a surge of prejudice and discrimination. Many were unfairly blamed for the spread of the virus and subjected to verbal abuse, physical attacks, and social ostracism. This backlash was fueled by misinformation and a lack of understanding, reflecting how fear and ignorance can exacerbate xenophobia and racism.

These examples highlight how quickly society can fall into the trap of stereotyping and prejudice when faced with fear or unfamiliarity. However, they also underscore the importance of promoting understanding and empathy.

I have observed that their perspectives often shift when individuals step out of their comfort zones and engage with people from different backgrounds, cultures, or lifestyles. This exposure plays a critical role in breaking down the walls of prejudice. It allows one to see beyond superficial differences and realize that, at our core, we share much in common. Regardless of our appearance, background, or beliefs, we all experience the same spectrum of emotions—joy, sadness, fear, and love.

Engaging with diverse groups can be transformative. It opens opportunities to learn about different ways of life, hear new stories, and understand distinct cultural viewpoints. This interaction fosters empathy and compassion as it becomes more apparent that the narratives we've been fed about 'the other' are often incomplete or inaccurate.

Moreover, this exposure helps to debunk the myths and

misconceptions that fuel stereotypes. It reveals the rich complexity of human experience, showing that no one can be neatly categorized into a single, oversimplified image. People are multifaceted, and their identities are shaped by many factors, much more than their racial, cultural, religious, or social attributes.

In teaching this lesson of exposure and understanding, I advocate for creating more opportunities for meaningful interactions across different groups. It's about building bridges of understanding, encouraging curiosity, and fostering an environment where diversity is tolerated and celebrated. This is crucial to creating a more inclusive, empathetic, and harmonious society in a vitality stage.

Furthermore, in my professional experience, I've observed scenarios where decision-makers are accused of discrimination. This includes racial discrimination, where individuals are treated differently based on their race or ethnicity. Gender discrimination is another prevalent issue, where decisions are biased against individuals based on their gender, often disadvantaging women or non-binary individuals. Age discrimination also occurs, particularly against older employees who may be unfairly passed over for promotions or job opportunities.

Additionally, there is discrimination based on sexual orientation, where LGBTQ+ individuals face biases and prejudices in workplace decisions. Religious discrimination is another area where individuals are unfairly treated due to their religious beliefs or practices. Disability discrimination, where individuals with disabilities are not provided with reasonable accommodations or are overlooked for opportunities, is also a significant concern. Socio-economic discrimination involves biases against individuals from lower socio-economic backgrounds, impacting their access to opportunities and resources. Furthermore, reverse discrimination occurs when policies intended to correct historical injustices inadvertently disadvantage individuals from traditionally dominant groups, creating a complex dynamic in efforts to promote equality and fairness.

These forms of discrimination by decision-makers can profoundly impact individuals and contribute to systemic inequalities across various sectors.

While these allegations can sometimes be valid, a closer examination often reveals a subtler yet pervasive issue – the impact of limited life experiences on decision-making.

Those responsible for selecting candidates for jobs, educational opportunities, or club memberships often don't consciously intend to discriminate. However, they may subconsciously gravitate towards what is familiar and comfortable, a tendency deeply rooted in their life experiences. This inclination can lead to unconscious biases that influence their decisions, resulting in unequal evaluations based on race, gender, socioeconomic background, or alma mater rather than solely on merit and qualifications.

Humans are primarily shaped by their experiences, and when these experiences are limited—particularly in terms of diversity—there is a natural, albeit unconscious, tendency to favor candidates who mirror their backgrounds, beliefs, or previous positive encounters. For instance, if a selector has had a negative experience with a particular demographic, they might, without realizing it, develop a bias against candidates from that group. These biases often result from limited exposure to diversity, fostering a preference for candidates who resemble the selector's experiences and perspectives.

This subconscious bias isn't always about overt prejudice; more often, it's about the comfort of familiarity. People tend to feel more at ease with what they know and understand, which can inadvertently lead to a homogenous selection. Additionally, choosing a candidate who aligns with familiar patterns can be considered a safe decision, potentially relieving the selector from future issues related to their choice.

Understanding this, it becomes clear that expanding one's experiences and exposure to diverse cultures, viewpoints, and backgrounds is crucial in a professional setting. It helps develop a more holistic perspective and a deeper understanding of different individuals. This broader exposure can break down subconscious biases and open up decision-makers to a more comprehensive range of candidates based on merit and potential rather than familiarity.

Andrew J. Scott, a professor of economics at the London Business School, succinctly captured a profound shift in the labor market with his statement: "As machines get better at being machines, humans have to get better at being more human. So human empathy, EQ, et cetera, will all become more important for employment." This quote underscores a critical trend in the automation and artificial intelligence (AI) age, where the nature of work and the skills required are evolving rapidly.

Emotional intelligence, often referred to as EQ (Emotional Quotient), is the ability to recognize, understand, and manage one's own emotions and those of others. It is a critical component of effective communication, relationship-building, and leadership.

In the past, technological advancements primarily replaced physical labor. Machines took over tasks that required human muscles, leading to the automation of many manual jobs. However, with the rise of AI and sophisticated algorithms, even cognitive tasks are increasingly being performed by machines. Computers now analyze vast amounts of data, perform complex calculations, and even engage in activities like diagnosing medical conditions or making financial decisions, tasks that once required human intellect.

This transition means that many traditional job functions are being automated, leading to concerns about job displacement. However, it also highlights a crucial area where humans still hold an advantage: emotional intelligence (EQ). Humans can understand and manage emotions, show empathy, and build relationships, unlike machines. These human-centric skills are becoming increasingly valuable in the workplace.

In fields such as healthcare, education, and customer service, the ability to connect with others on a personal level is irreplaceable. For instance, while AI can assist doctors by providing data-driven insights, it cannot replace the compassion and empathy required to comfort a patient. Similarly, teachers use emotional intelligence to inspire and motivate students, something that machines cannot replicate.

Furthermore, as organizations strive to create more inclusive and dynamic work environments, teamwork, leadership, and communication skills are more critical than ever. These attributes foster collaboration and innovation, driving business success in ways automated systems cannot.

The growing emphasis on these human-centric skills reflects a broader societal trend toward valuing emotional well-being and mental health. Ensuring employees feel valued and understood becomes crucial for maintaining morale and productivity as workplaces become more automated.

Andrew J. Scott's observation highlights a pivotal shift in the job market. As machines take over more technical and analytical tasks, the distinctively human qualities of empathy, emotional intelligence, and interpersonal skills are becoming increasingly essential. This shift influences employment trends and underscores the enduring value of human connection and emotional insight in an increasingly automated world.

As we navigate a world increasingly dominated by technology, where machines and automated systems perform many tasks previously handled by humans, emotional intelligence emerges as a distinctly human advantage over automated machines. This ability to recognize, understand, and manage our own emotions and those of others remains uniquely human. Emotional intelligence encompasses several critical skills, including empathy, emotional regulation, and the ability to navigate social complexities, which are not easily replicated by artificial intelligence.

Emotional intelligence is pivotal in various aspects of our life and work. High emotional intelligence is linked to better leadership, teamwork, and communication abilities in professional settings. It enables individuals to resolve conflicts more effectively, foster a collaborative work environment, and lead others with understanding and inspiration. In personal contexts, emotional intelligence enhances relationships, promoting more profound understanding and stronger bonds between individuals.

Given the rapid advancement of AI and automation, there is a growing emphasis on cultivating and enhancing these emotional competencies. While machines excel at processing and executing tasks quickly and efficiently, they still lack the nuanced emotional understanding that comes naturally to humans. This gap suggests that roles requiring high levels of emotional intelligence will likely remain in human hands for the foreseeable future, underscoring the importance of developing these skills.

As technology reshapes the labor landscape, the demand for emotional intelligence could increase as its value in fostering human-centric environments becomes more apparent. Emphasizing emotional intelligence in education, training programs, and professional development can prepare individuals for a future where social skills and emotional insight are more critical than ever. Thus, not only should we continue to use and value our emotional intelligence, but we should also actively seek to develop and improve it to maintain our relevance in this evolving world.

Turning the Tide: Navigating the Challenges of Climate Change

"Impossible is not a fact, it's an attitude. It's only an attitude, and attitudes are changeable." - Christiana Figueres

Throughout my tenure at NASA and later with INNOVIM, I collaborated with some of the foremost Earth scientists. My initial expertise lay in designing and developing complex data systems to manage, analyze, and visualize climate data for various Earth mission projects. Later, I transitioned to forming a company heavily involved in climate science, supporting NASA and the National Oceanic and Atmospheric Administration (NOAA). The innovative technologies we develop play a crucial role in processing and interpreting immense volumes of data collected from satellites, ground stations, and other observational tools. This data is vital for understanding and addressing climate change, enabling scientists to make informed decisions and advance our knowledge of Earth's systems.

My involvement in these projects has given me a unique perspective on the vast and intricate data about our planet's climate. Working alongside experts who study atmospheric conditions, ocean temperatures, ice cover, and other critical environmental indicators, I have gained a deeper understanding of the significant changes occurring in our climate system. The data unequivocally show trends such as rising global temperatures, increasing frequency of extreme weather events, shrinking ice caps, and rising sea levels. These observations underscore the reality and urgency of climate change.

For instance, data from NASA's Earth observation satellites have shown that the last decade was the warmest, with 2016 and 2020 tied for the hottest years ever recorded. This warming trend is primarily attributed to the increased concentrations of greenhouse gases such as carbon dioxide, methane, and nitrous oxide, resulting from human activities like fossil fuel combustion, deforestation, and industrial processes.

By designing and developing complex and mission-critical data systems for NASA and NOAA, we have contributed to Earth scientists' efforts by ensuring they have the innovative technology tools to monitor these changes accurately and predict future climate scenarios. The insights gained from analyzing this data are critical for informing policymakers, guiding mitigation strategies, and raising public awareness about the need for urgent action to combat climate change.

Being exposed to this wealth of climate data has profoundly impacted my understanding of our environmental challenges. It has reinforced the importance of scientific research and technological innovation in addressing one of the most pressing issues of our time. My experiences have opened my eyes to the stark realities of climate change and fueled my commitment to leveraging data and technology to support sustainable solutions for a healthier planet.

Within the vast chronicles of human understanding, numerous truths have emerged, each hard-fought and often met with the skepticism that defines our historical journey. From the revelation of Earth's spherical form to the complex ballet of planets in our solar system and the hidden realms of microscopic pathogens to the expansive and intricate web of genetic inheritance, our path to discovery has been marked by a continuous interplay of resistance and enlightenment. Each groundbreaking insight has marked a pivotal transition from doubt to acknowledgment, illustrating the resilience and curiosity inherent in the human spirit. This journey, replete with challenges and triumphs, underscores our relentless quest for knowledge and our ability to reshape our comprehension of the universe.

Throughout the chronicles of scientific exploration, each significant breakthrough has frequently confronted a tide of skepticism and resistance. These pivotal moments of discovery have relentlessly challenged established paradigms, transforming our grasp of the world around us. With each significant revelation, however, voices of opposition have emerged, reflecting a persistent undercurrent of ignorance, even amidst burgeoning knowledge. This hesitance to embrace new concepts often stems from deeply rooted religious beliefs, entrenched conventional wisdom, or a fundamental fear of the unknown. Such reluctance is a striking reminder of the human inclination to favor the security of familiar views, underscoring the complex interplay between knowledge, belief, and resistance to change. This dynamic illustrates a barrier to scientific progress and a critical aspect of our collective journey toward understanding and enlightenment.

In the contemporary landscape, the challenge of climate change stands as a stark testament to the ongoing clash between personal beliefs and scientific facts. As a fervent proponent of objective inquiry, my involvement in this crucial discourse is anchored in a firm conviction that reliance on peer-reviewed research and an unwavering commitment to scientific precision is indispensable in confronting these global predicaments. Although science is never absolute, and knowledge evolves with the latest findings and data, it is through this rigorous process that we can effectively address the pressing issues of our time.

My role has been multifaceted; it entails comprehending the intricacies of climate data and actively engaging in the broader dialogue. By advocating for informed, evidence-based strategies, I aim to contribute to a more nuanced understanding and effective response to the complex and pressing issue of climate change. This commitment reflects a dedication to bridging the gap between knowledge and action, emphasizing the necessity of grounding our approaches in solid scientific foundations to foster meaningful and sustainable change.

The debate on climate change sharply delineates the divide between science deniers and the scientific community. Those denying the science tend to base their arguments on subjective interpretations, personal beliefs, and emotional responses, often disregarding empirical evidence. On the other hand, scientists and engineers approach the issue with a foundation of objectivity, grounding their analyses and conclusions in verifiable facts, precise measurements, and observable phenomena.

This systematic and evidence-based approach is vital in navigating the complexities of climate change. It ensures that our understanding of the issue is rooted in empirical data and factual accuracy, which are critical for making informed decisions and devising effective, realistic solutions. Recognizing and addressing this divide is crucial in fostering a more informed public discourse and progressing toward meaningful action against climate change.

Despite some contention over human influence on climate patterns, the preponderance of evidence creates a compelling narrative. While it's true that the Earth's climate undergoes natural cycles, the current phase of climate change, bolstered by decades of meticulous peer-reviewed research, stands apart in its clarity and urgency. The terms "climate change" or "global warming" are more than just labels; they encapsulate a global phenomenon that transcends national and geographic boundaries.

Indeed, over the last several hundred thousand years, Earth has experienced numerous cycles of gradual cooling and rapid global warming, significantly impacting its geological and environmental landscape. Various factors have driven these climatic shifts, including changes in Earth's orbit, solar radiation, volcanic activity, and greenhouse gas concentrations. Additionally, variations in Earth's magnetic field have also had an impact, albeit more indirectly. Changes in the magnetic field can influence the distribution and intensity of solar radiation reaching Earth's surface, which in turn can affect climate patterns.

This interplay of multiple factors underscores the complexity of Earth's climate system and the numerous forces that can drive significant environmental changes. These natural cycles have shaped the planet's ecosystems and influenced the evolution and migration of human populations.

The most recent ice age, known as the Last Glacial Maximum, peaked around 20,000 years ago when vast ice sheets covered significant portions of North America, Europe, and Asia. This period was characterized by colder temperatures and lower sea levels, creating land bridges that allowed early humans and other species to migrate across continents. Approximately 11,700 years ago, the Earth began transitioning out of this ice age during a period known as the Holocene epoch. This transition marked a phase of rapid global warming, leading to the retreat of glaciers and rising sea levels.

The rapid warming that followed the last ice age profoundly affected the planet's geology and environment, creating conditions favorable for human survival and the development of civilizations. As the ice sheets melted, they released vast amounts of water, reshaping coastlines and forming new rivers and lakes. The warmer climate also facilitated the expansion of forests and grasslands, providing abundant resources for hunter-gatherer societies. This period saw significant advancements in human technology and culture, as stable climates allowed for the development of agriculture and the establishment of permanent settlements.

The increased availability of diverse flora and fauna also supported the flourishing of human societies during this post-glacial warming period. As ecosystems rebounded, humans could exploit various food sources, leading to population growth and the development of complex social structures. This era laid the groundwork for the rise of early civilizations, such as those in Mesopotamia, the Indus Valley, and ancient Egypt, which emerged as humans began to domesticate plants and animals and develop sophisticated tools and techniques for agriculture.

The cycles of ice ages and subsequent warming periods have been crucial in shaping the Earth's environment and the course of human history. The end of the last ice age, in particular, played a pivotal role in creating the conditions necessary for human societies to thrive, demonstrating the profound interconnectedness between climate and the development of life on Earth.

The tangible effects, such as the retreat of glaciers and the warming of the atmosphere and the oceans, offer stark, visible proof of the issue's severity. These manifestations allow even skeptics to witness firsthand the scale of the problem. While there may be ongoing debates about the extent of human contribution, the empirical data leaves no room for doubt about the reality of climate change and its widespread impacts. This data not only underscores the gravity of the situation but also emphasizes the critical need for informed action based on scientific understanding.

The effects of global warming, a central component of climate change, are wide-ranging and significant. The increase in global temperatures amplifies various environmental issues. One of the most noticeable impacts is the warming of the oceans, which affects marine ecosystems and alters weather patterns globally. Warmer oceans contribute to more intense hurricanes and typhoons, disrupt marine biodiversity, and affect the livelihoods of communities dependent on fishing and tourism. This increased heat content leads to more frequent and severe weather events, further stressing the importance of addressing climate change comprehensively.

We are witnessing more severe hurricanes, prolonged droughts, and intense heat waves than ever. These events have direct and often devastating consequences for communities worldwide, affecting agriculture, water resources, human health, and habitation, with vulnerable populations being hit the hardest.

In 2024, heat waves highlighted the ongoing impacts of climate change. Countries like Greece, Cyprus, Turkey, and Italy experienced temperatures soaring 18°F (10°C) above the seasonal average, causing widespread disruptions and concerns for public health and safety. These regions, along with many others, are not accustomed to such high temperatures and often lack basic comforts such as air conditioning, exacerbating the effects of the heat.

Africa and the Middle East have also experienced record-breaking temperatures. For instance, parts of the Middle East, including Iraq and Kuwait, saw temperatures surpassing 122°F (50°C). Heat waves have severe consequences for vulnerable populations, including the elderly, children, and individuals with chronic illnesses. For example, New York City reported increasing heat-related deaths, disproportionately affecting lower-income and historically underserved communities. The risk of heat-related illnesses such as heat exhaustion and heat stroke is significant, particularly in areas without adequate cooling infrastructure.

Climate change and global warming also significantly increase the frequency and intensity of forest fires worldwide. Higher temperatures and more extreme weather patterns lead to longer fire seasons and more severe fires, particularly in northern regions like Canada and Russia. In 2023, Canada experienced its worst wildfire season on record, burning millions of hectares and releasing massive amounts of carbon dioxide, exacerbating global warming.

In the United States, the western states, including California, Oregon, and Washington, have seen a marked increase in wildfire activity. Climate change has led to hotter, drier conditions, creating an environment ripe for fires. For instance, California has had unprecedented fire alerts in recent years, resulting in extensive burnt areas.

South America has also been affected, with Chile experiencing devastating wildfires in early 2023. These fires, driven by high temperatures and dry conditions, caused significant loss of life and property and contributed to global carbon emissions.

Forest fires have significantly impacted Indonesia in Asia, particularly during the El Niño events, which bring drier weather conditions. In 2023, Indonesia experienced its driest weather since 2019, resulting in intense fires in regions like Sumatra and Kalimantan. These fires led to severe air pollution, affecting air quality across the country and beyond. Additionally, countries in the upper ASEAN region, such as Thailand and Myanmar, saw increased fire activity, leading to elevated levels of particulate matter and deteriorating air quality.

Although not traditionally associated with forest fires, the Middle East has seen an increase in wildfires due to rising temperatures and prolonged droughts. In Turkey, the summer of 2021 saw some of the worst wildfires in the country's history, burning thousands of hectares of forest and farmland. Extreme heatwaves and dry conditions exacerbated the fires. Similarly, in Israel, wildfires have become more frequent and intense, often driven by extreme weather conditions and arid landscapes.

In Africa, the impact of climate change on forest fires is evident in several regions. For instance, in 2020, Angola and the Democratic Republic of Congo experienced many wildfires. These fires were fueled by high temperatures and dry conditions, often linked to climate change. Additionally, in the savannah regions of Southern Africa, countries like Zimbabwe and Zambia have seen an increase in the frequency and intensity of wildfires, which devastate large tracts of land and disrupt local ecosystems.

The impact of these forest fires on humanity is severe and multifaceted. They lead to the direct loss of life and property, displace communities, and cause long-term health issues due to smoke and poor air quality. The carbon emissions from these fires further exacerbate global warming, creating a vicious cycle that leads to even more severe climate conditions and increased fire risks.

Climate change also significantly impacts animal migrations in Africa, as the World Economic Forum and National Geographic noted. Changes in rainfall patterns and increasing temperatures disrupt the availability of water and grazing land, affecting the timing and routes of these migrations. Prolonged droughts, for example, can alter migratory routes and timing, leading to cascading effects on the entire ecosystem.

The largest animal migration in Africa is the annual wildebeest migration, where over 1.5 million wildebeest, accompanied by hundreds of thousands of zebras and gazelles, travel across the Serengeti-Mara ecosystem. Seasonal rains drive this migration as the animals search for fresh grazing land and water. Climate change leads to unpredictable rainfall patterns, higher temperatures, and extended droughts, all of which impact the availability of resources essential for these animals' survival. Consequently, migratory patterns are disrupted, causing malnutrition, increased predation risk, and potential declines in population sizes.

This disruption stresses the migrating animals and affects the ecological balance of the Serengeti-Mara ecosystem. These migrations are crucial for seed distribution, soil fertilization, and maintaining predator-prey dynamics. Addressing climate change is essential to preserving these natural processes and ensuring the survival of migratory species. The interconnectedness of these migrations highlights the importance of global efforts to mitigate climate change and protect biodiversity.

Insects are also significantly impacted by climate change, which disrupts their life cycles and habitats. For instance, climate change disrupts the life cycles of butterflies by altering migration, breeding, and food availability, leading to mismatches with nectar plants and threatening their survival. For bees, rising temperatures and extreme weather events disrupt foraging patterns and colony health, resulting in declining populations and impacting crop yields and food production. Other insects, like dragonflies and beetles, face habitat changes and life cycle disruptions, with some pests expanding their range and causing more crop damage, while beneficial insects struggle to adapt.

These changes threaten biodiversity and disrupt entire ecosystems, with cascading effects on other wildlife and plant species. The decline of insect populations has profound implications for humans, including reduced pollination, lower crop yields, higher food prices, and increased spread of crop diseases and vector-borne illnesses. This underscores the interconnectedness of all life forms and the urgent need for climate action to protect natural ecosystems and human well-being.

Global warming also impacts ocean coral ecosystems, which are crucial for marine biodiversity. Coral reefs are susceptible to changes in water temperature. When ocean temperatures rise, corals experience stress and expel the symbiotic algae (zooxanthellae) that live within their tissues. This process, known as coral bleaching, causes the corals to turn white and significantly reduces their ability to photosynthesize, ultimately leading to their death if the stressful conditions persist.

The Great Barrier Reef in Australia has recently experienced severe bleaching, with the 2023-2024 event particularly devastating. Unprecedented marine heatwaves affected large reef areas, causing widespread bleaching and highlighting the urgent need for effective climate action to protect this biodiversity hotspot.

In 2023, the reefs in Florida, USA, experienced severe bleaching, with conditions starting earlier and lasting longer than in previous events. This prolonged heat stress significantly damaged the coral populations, emphasizing the increasing vulnerability of these ecosystems to rising ocean temperatures.

Across the Caribbean Sea, coral reefs in countries like Mexico, El Salvador, Costa Rica, Panama, Colombia, and Brazil have suffered extensive bleaching due to high sea temperatures. These events have stressed vital marine ecosystems, crucial for the biodiversity and economies of these regions.

Significant coral bleaching has been reported in the South Pacific Islands, including Fiji, Vanuatu, Tuvalu, Kiribati, the Samoas, and French Polynesia. These islands rely heavily on coral reefs for coastal protection and local economies, making the impact of bleaching events particularly severe.

The Red Sea, including the Gulf of Aqaba, has also experienced severe bleaching. Although some coral species have shown resilience, the increasing temperature trends pose a significant threat to these ecosystems, which are vital for marine biodiversity in the region.

Coral reefs in the Persian Gulf have been subjected to extreme heat stress, leading to extensive bleaching. The harsh conditions in this region make the reefs especially susceptible to temperature changes, threatening the delicate balance of these marine environments.

In the Indian Ocean, areas such as Tanzania, Kenya, Mauritius, the Seychelles, Tromelin, Mayotte, and parts of Indonesia have reported coral bleaching events. These regions are critical for marine biodiversity and support the livelihoods of many coastal communities.

The consequences of coral bleaching extend far beyond the corals themselves. Coral reefs are often called the "rainforests of the sea" due to their incredible biodiversity. They provide habitat, food, and breeding grounds for approximately 25% of all marine species, including fish, crustaceans, and mollusks. The loss of coral reefs due to bleaching disrupts these ecosystems, leading to a decline in marine species diversity and abundance.

Furthermore, coral reefs play a critical role in coastal protection. They act as natural barriers, reducing the impact of waves, storms, and erosion on coastal communities. Therefore, the degradation of coral reefs affects marine life and human populations that depend on these ecosystems for food, tourism, and coastal protection.

Additionally, coral reefs contribute to global carbon cycling. Healthy corals sequester carbon dioxide, helping mitigate climate change's effects. As coral reefs decline, their capacity to act as carbon sinks diminishes, exacerbating global warming.

The impact of global warming on coral reefs is another clear example of how climate change can have cascading effects on biodiversity and ecosystem services.

Water management is poised to become one of the most

critical issues facing the global community in the coming years. As climate change intensifies, we will likely encounter extreme disparities in water availability. Some regions will grapple with severe droughts as rivers dry up and groundwater reserves deplete, leading to further environmental instability such as land subsidence. Conversely, other areas may suffer from excessive rainfall, resulting in devastating floods that overwhelm people and infrastructure. These contrasting challenges underscore the urgent need for effective water management strategies. Such strategies will be essential in our efforts to adapt to and mitigate the impacts of climate change, ensuring sustainable water resources for future generations.

Water conflicts, increasingly known as "water wars," are becoming more prevalent as global warming intensifies, exacerbating water scarcity across the globe. Rising temperatures and shifting climate patterns lead to uneven rainfall distribution, prolonged droughts, and reduced snowpacks, crucial freshwater sources for many regions. These environmental changes strain the precarious balance of water resource management, heightening tensions between countries that share water basins.

In the Middle East and North Africa, two of the most water-scarce regions in the world, countries like Iraq, Jordan, Syria, and Israel face severe challenges over shared resources such as the Tigris, Euphrates, and Jordan rivers. Climate change threatens to alter these rivers' flow patterns and availability, potentially increasing conflict risks as nations compete for diminishing supplies. Additionally, the construction of dams by upstream countries has become a contentious issue, as these structures can significantly reduce water flow to downstream nations, exacerbating tensions and disputes over water rights.

Turkey's control over the headwaters of the Tigris and Euphrates rivers places it in a powerful position regarding water resources, affecting Iraq and Syria. Turkey's Southeastern Anatolia Project (GAP), an extensive development project involving the construction of 22 dams and 19 hydroelectric power plants, has significantly reduced water flow to these downstream countries. Iraq and Syria, heavily dependent on the Euphrates and Tigris for their agricultural and domestic water needs, view the GAP as a direct threat to their water security. The reduced river flow exacerbates existing water scarcity, heightening tensions and compounding challenges related to agriculture, drinking water supplies, and ecological health.

Iran and Afghanistan share several rivers, most notably the Helmand River, which originates in the Hindu Kush mountains of Afghanistan. Water conflicts have escalated due to Afghanistan's plans to harness these rivers for irrigation and hydroelectric projects, notably the Kajaki Dam on the Helmand River. These developments threaten to reduce the water flow into Iran, a country already grappling with severe water shortages due to prolonged droughts, over-extraction of groundwater, and inefficient agricultural practices.

Similarly, in Central Asia, the republics of Kazakhstan, Kyrgyzstan, Tajikistan, Uzbekistan, and Turkmenistan grapple with the impacts of glacial melt and changing precipitation on the Syr Darya and Amu Darya rivers, vital for their agricultural and energy sectors. Dam building, while crucial for energy production and water storage, often restricts water availability to downstream countries, leading to disputes over water sharing.

Further south, the Grand Ethiopian Renaissance Dam (GERD) on the Blue Nile is a significant example of how climate-induced changes and infrastructure projects complicate negotiations. Ethiopia, Sudan, and Egypt are locked in a tripartite dispute over the dam's impact on water flows to the Nile, a lifeline to all three countries, especially Egypt, which relies on the Nile for most of its water needs.

The situation is similarly dire in Africa's Lake Chad Basin, where Cameroon, Chad, Niger, and Nigeria witness the lake shrinking dramatically due to increased evaporation rates and higher water usage, which fuel conflicts over the remaining resources. The construction of dams in this region further complicates the distribution and availability of water, leading to intensified disputes among the basin countries.

CURRENTS OF BEING

The Colorado River Basin exemplifies the internal conflicts stemming from climate change in the United States. The river serves seven states and Mexico, all facing increasing water shortages and legal disputes as the river's flow decreases due to prolonged droughts linked to global warming. The situation is aggravated by dam projects that regulate and reroute water for urban and agricultural use, often at the expense of downstream users. The construction of dams along the Colorado River has led to disputes between upstream and downstream states. These dams are crucial for providing water for agriculture, urban areas, and hydropower, but they also limit water availability for downstream states, leading to conflicts over water rights and allocation.

Similarly, in China, the construction of numerous dams on rivers like the Yangtze and Mekong has led to domestic and international tensions over water distribution and environmental impact.

These examples illustrate the complex interplay between climate change, infrastructure projects, and water resource management, underscoring the critical importance of international cooperation and sustainable water management strategies. As global warming intensifies, water becomes an increasingly scarce commodity, heightening the potential for conflicts. Therefore, regions and countries must adapt and mitigate these effects through collaborative efforts and innovative solutions to ensure equitable water distribution and minimize disputes.

The escalation of sea levels, precipitated by the dual phenomena of warming oceans and the melting of polar ice caps, presents a formidable challenge, particularly to coastal areas. This rise in sea levels places low-lying regions in the direct path of danger, with the looming threat of submersion becoming increasingly imminent. The consequences are far-reaching: extensive flooding becomes a reality, leading to the displacement of large populations.

This forced migration to higher, safer grounds is not a simple relocation; it is a disruption that ripples through communities, tearing at the fabric of established ways of life. The impact extends beyond the immediately affected areas, as the influx of displaced populations into new regions strains already limited resources. This can lead to heightened socio-economic disparities as resources become scarce and competition for them intensifies.

This situation presents significant challenges to existing infrastructures and governance systems. Infrastructure designed for a different era and set of circumstances may need to be revised in the face of these new demands, requiring substantial adaptation and redevelopment. Governance systems are also tested, as they must address the immediate humanitarian needs and the longer-term implications of population displacement, resource allocation, and community integration.

Rising sea levels due to global warming are an environmental concern and a complex socio-economic challenge that requires comprehensive, forward-thinking, and sustainable solutions. They underscore the interconnectedness of our global community and the need for cooperative, coordinated responses to address the multifaceted impacts of climate change. The intricate dynamics highlight the critical necessity for a collective and determined global response. Tackling the challenges posed by global warming calls for an all-encompassing strategy that spans various domains and sectors.

Implementing sustainable practices is essential in this effort. This includes transitioning to renewable energy sources, promoting energy efficiency, and adopting sustainable land use and agricultural practices. Such initiatives reduce greenhouse gas emissions and encourage a more harmonious relationship with our environment.

Another critical aspect is investing in resilient infrastructure. This involves designing and constructing buildings, transportation networks, and other infrastructures that withstand the changing climate and extreme weather events. Such investments are crucial in safeguarding communities, particularly those in vulnerable regions, from the immediate physical impacts of climate change.

Moreover, fostering international cooperation is

indispensable. Climate change is a global issue that knows no borders. Coordinated action, shared resources, and knowledge transfer between nations are vital for effective mitigation and adaptation strategies. This cooperation should also aim to support less developed countries, which are often the most affected by climate change yet the least equipped to deal with its consequences.

However, the challenge of achieving such cooperation is evident in the reluctance of some developing countries to participate fully in international climate agreements. For instance, countries like China, India, and Brazil have sometimes hesitated to commit to stringent emissions reductions. Given their development status, these nations argue that their primary focus must be economic growth and poverty alleviation. They contend that developed countries, which have historically contributed the most to greenhouse gas emissions, should bear a larger share of the responsibility for climate action.

China, the world's largest emitter of carbon dioxide, has made significant strides in renewable energy but often resists binding international commitments that could hamper its economic growth. Similarly, while investing heavily in solar energy, India still relies extensively on coal to meet its energy needs. It has argued for a more equitable distribution of emissions reduction targets considering historical emissions. Brazil, home to the critical Amazon rainforest, has faced international criticism for deforestation rates under policies prioritizing agricultural expansion and economic development.

Brazil, home to the vital Amazon rainforest, has faced international criticism for deforestation rates driven by agricultural expansion and economic development. The Amazon is essential for the global climate because it stores a vast amount of carbon, helping to stabilize global temperatures by absorbing carbon dioxide from the atmosphere. Additionally, the Amazon releases significant amounts of water into the atmosphere daily through evapotranspiration, influencing weather patterns and the global water cycle.

However, deforestation in the Amazon is increasing due to logging, mining, and the expansion of agricultural lands. This releases stored carbon back into the atmosphere and disrupts crucial ecological processes. The loss of forest cover can lead to increased temperatures and altered precipitation patterns, potentially transforming the rainforest into a savanna-like ecosystem.

Efforts to combat this include promoting sustainable land use practices, reforestation projects, and enforcing environmental protection laws. Preserving the Amazon is a global imperative, highlighting the interconnectedness of our environment and the need for coordinated efforts to mitigate climate change and protect natural ecosystems.

These examples underscore the complexity of achieving global consensus on climate action. Developed nations must recognize the developmental needs of these countries and provide support through financial aid, technology transfer, and capacity-building initiatives. Through such cooperative and equitable approaches, meaningful global progress can be made in combating climate change.

A failure to act comprehensively and decisively could worsen environmental degradation and amplify social inequalities. This, in turn, jeopardizes the welfare of the current population and future generations. Thus, addressing climate change is a matter of environmental stewardship and a moral imperative to ensure a livable and equitable world.

The Gaia hypothesis, formulated by James Lovelock and Lynn Margulis in the 1970s, conceptualizes Earth as a self-regulating organism. Its biological and physical components are interlinked to sustain conditions conducive to life. This theory proposes that Earth inherently moderates critical variables like climate and ocean salinity to maintain its habitability.

This perspective is fascinating but requires a more detailed and scientific understanding to fully grasp how Earth responds to anthropogenic environmental changes, such as climate change, and their impact on human lives. For example, while volcanic eruptions do affect the climate by releasing large amounts of ash and sulfur dioxide into the stratosphere—which can reflect sunlight and induce temporary cooling, as seen with the 1991 eruption of Mount Pinatubo in the Philippines that temporarily lowered global temperatures by about 0.6 degrees Celsius (1.1 degrees Fahrenheit)—these are natural geological processes driven by Earth's internal dynamics, not deliberate corrective responses to human activity. Moreover, these cooling effects are transient, whereas greenhouse gases like carbon dioxide contribute to a longer-term warming of the planet.

While the Gaia hypothesis suggests that Earth might eventually self-correct, the mechanisms and outcomes of such processes remain uncertain, especially in the context of rapid environmental changes induced by human activity. How these potential corrections would affect human life needs to be clarified, and whether they could counterbalance the extensive changes already set in motion.

This uncertainty underscores the need for a deeper exploration of Earth's complex system responses and the implications for future environmental stability and human survival. A thorough scientific understanding is essential to appreciate the complexities of Earth's response to human-induced environmental changes and to develop strategies to safeguard both the planet and human well-being. This holistic approach combines rigorous data analysis with innovative solutions to address the multifaceted challenges of climate change.

The fast rise in extreme weather events, such as hurricanes, droughts, and heavy rainfall, is more directly attributable to climate change driven by human-induced increases in greenhouse gases. Global temperature rises to enhance water evaporation, resulting in heavier precipitation in some areas and dryer conditions in others. These phenomena may seem like the Earth responding to atmospheric alterations, but they are not intentional, self-regulating actions by the planet; instead, they are consequences of changed atmospheric conditions.

Earth's systems naturally evolve over geological timescales, including through ice ages and significant climatic and atmospheric shifts. These long-term changes, driven by factors like solar radiation variations, continental drift, and volcanic activity, are part of Earth's natural cycles, not responses to human impact. These processes operate over durations much more extended than human timescales, underscoring the complexity of Earth's dynamic systems independent of immediate human influences.

While the Gaia hypothesis offers an intriguing way to think about Earth's complexity and interdependent systems, the current scientific understanding suggests that Earth does not act as a sentient organism that intentionally responds to human impacts. Instead, the changes we observe in climate and weather patterns result from Earth's natural systems interacting with significant alterations we have made to the atmosphere and environment. The responsibility to address and mitigate these changes lies with us, requiring concerted global efforts in environmental protection, sustainable practices, and reduction of greenhouse gas emissions.

SHAHIN SAMADI

Crossing Thresholds: Journeys of Hope and New Beginnings

"When we least expect it, life sets us a challenge to test our courage and willingness to change; at such a moment, there is no point in pretending that nothing has happened or in saying that we are not yet ready. The challenge will not wait. Life does not look back." - Paulo Coelho

In 1976, I moved to the United States at a young age to pursue my education. Following the 1979 Iranian Revolution, I decided not to return to Iran. Fortunately, America, my second home, offered numerous opportunities and support, allowing me to build a new life. I have spent my entire adult life here, receiving my education, building my career, and starting my family. While I hold my Persian heritage with great pride, I also consider myself a proud American and am profoundly grateful for the countless opportunities this country has afforded me. My journey is a testament to the resilience and adaptability of immigrants who enrich their adopted homelands while maintaining a deep connection to their roots.

Throughout history, people have migrated from one place to another or from one country to another, driven by the hope of a better life or the desire to transform their current circumstances. This movement, often fueled by aspirations for improved economic opportunities, safety, and stability, reflects a profound human pursuit of progress and security. Whether escaping adverse conditions or seeking new horizons, immigrants' journeys are a testament to their resilience and determination to forge a more promising future for themselves and their families.

Many countries have opened their doors to immigrants, offering them opportunities that were unavailable in their home countries. This gesture of hospitality has enabled millions to access better educational prospects, enhanced economic possibilities, and safer living conditions. Nations with inclusive immigration policies recognize the mutual benefits of diversity and the contributions immigrants can bring to society—enriching cultural landscapes, invigorating economies, and fostering global connections. These welcoming countries serve as new homes for immigrants and beacons of hope for those seeking change and improvement.

While many people travel to other countries for education or employment opportunities, recently, there has been a significant number of individuals and families undertaking dangerous journeys to Europe from the Middle East and Africa and from Latin America to the U.S. These migrants are driven by a desperate need to escape conflicts and severe poverty, in search of safety and better prospects. In the process, they leave their homes, possessions, and loved ones behind with high hopes and expectations for a new life. However, the arduous nature of their journey often leaves them little time or energy to consider the challenges that lie ahead.

After the outbreak of the Syrian Civil War in 2011, millions of Syrians were forced to flee their homes, seeking refuge in neighboring countries and Europe. During a visit to Europe, I was deeply touched to witness the plight of many refugees from the Middle East. Families who had endured unimaginable hardships were now panhandling on the streets, struggling to survive in their new surroundings. The sight of these displaced individuals, including children, reminded me of the ongoing humanitarian crisis and the urgent need for international support and compassion.

Immigration is a sensitive topic for the population of host countries, as it places significant demands on infrastructure and the job market. The influx of immigrants can strain public services such as healthcare, education, and housing, leading to concerns among citizens about resource allocation and availability. Additionally, the job market may become more competitive, with fears that immigrants might accept lower wages, potentially driving down overall wage levels and affecting job opportunities for the native population.

On the other hand, many immigrants dream of a better life in a new country, driven by the hope of escaping conflict, persecution, or economic hardship. However, upon arrival, they often face harsh realities that make achieving their aspirations difficult. Language barriers, cultural differences, and limited recognition of foreign qualifications can hinder their ability to integrate and secure stable employment. This can result in immigrants taking low-paying, unskilled jobs far below their qualifications and expectations. Additionally, immigrants frequently encounter discrimination and prejudice, which further complicates their efforts to build a new life. Such biases can manifest in various forms, from social exclusion and biased hiring practices to more overt acts of hostility, significantly impacting their ability to integrate and thrive in their new communities.

Upon reaching safer ground, the initial relief of achieving their goal is often quickly overshadowed by the difficulties of assimilating into an unfamiliar society. The challenges of adapting to new cultural norms, overcoming language barriers, and the frequent absence of a supportive network can be overwhelming. These migrants then face the daunting task of rebuilding their lives in an environment that is starkly different from what they knew, requiring significant resilience and determination to navigate their new reality.

Many spend months, sometimes even years, in refugee camps in transit countries before reaching their intended destinations. For some, the dream still needs to be fulfilled as they never manage to complete their journey. Often overcrowded and under-resourced, these camps become temporary homes where basic necessities such as shelter, food, and medical care are scarce. The prolonged uncertainty and the harsh conditions of these camps add to the physical and psychological strain on the refugees, complicating their aspirations for a stable and secure future.

Those who arrive in a new country without legal authorization often face harsh initial experiences. Vulnerable due to their status, they frequently fall victim to individuals or groups who exploit their situation. This exploitation can take various forms, including labor abuse, where they are forced to work under severe conditions for minimal pay; housing exploitation, where they are charged exorbitant rates for substandard living conditions; and other forms of manipulation and coercion.

This unfortunate reality often marks immigrants' first encounter with life in their new country, setting a challenging tone for their future. For instance, according to a 2018 Organization for Economic Co-operation and Development (OECD) report, many highly educated immigrants in European countries were employed in low-skilled jobs. This underutilization of skills affects the immigrants' economic well-being and represents a loss of potential economic contributions to the host country.

Furthermore, the emotional and psychological toll on immigrants can be significant. The experience of living in a new and unfamiliar environment, often with limited social support, can lead to feelings of isolation and stress. This is exacerbated by the uncertainty surrounding their legal status and the potential for discrimination or xenophobia.

In search of comfort and familiarity, many immigrants gravitate towards close-knit communities within the host country where they can speak their native language and maintain their cultural practices. These enclaves provide essential emotional and social support, helping immigrants cope with the challenges of adapting to a new environment. Cities like Berlin, Paris, and New York are well-known for their vibrant immigrant neighborhoods, which serve as cultural havens and offer a sense of home away from home. These communities provide a refuge where immigrants can preserve their traditions, celebrate their holidays, and support each other in their new lives.

However, the existence of these enclaves can sometimes hinder the broader integration process. The cultural ties within these communities can result in limited interaction with the broader society and slower acquisition of the host country's language and customs. For example, studies have shown that immigrants living in concentrated ethnic neighborhoods may have fewer opportunities to practice the local language, which can impede their language proficiency and integration into the broader workforce.

As immigrants become more comfortable within their

communities, some may attempt to promote their culture and religion to the local population. This can occasionally lead to tensions, particularly when cultural practices or religious observances contradict local norms.

In some European cities, such as London, Paris, and Berlin, there have been instances where Muslim immigrants perform Friday prayers in public spaces or advocate for changes to school curricula to accommodate Islamic teachings. These actions can be perceived as intrusive or offensive by residents, exacerbating cultural and religious divides and fueling anti-immigrant sentiments. In Paris, public prayers in the streets by Muslim communities have led to significant controversy and backlash, with critics arguing that such practices disrupt public order and infringe on the secular nature of the French state. Similarly, in Berlin, there have been debates over the inclusion of Islamic religious education in public schools, which some locals view as a challenge to the country's secular educational framework.

Systemic barriers compound integration challenges. According to a 2019 report by the Migration Policy Institute, many immigrants face difficulties accessing education, employment, and healthcare due to language barriers, legal restrictions, and discrimination. For example, immigrants who arrive in the United States without fluent English proficiency are less likely to find jobs that match their skill levels, contributing to economic disparities.

Furthermore, the need for recognition of foreign qualifications remains a significant issue. The OECD has noted that immigrants often work in jobs below their skill level, which affects their economic stability and results in a substantial loss of potential economic contributions to the host country. This underemployment is a persistent issue across many developed nations, leading to the inefficient utilization of human capital.

These challenges highlight the urgent need for comprehensive policies that address the recognition of foreign qualifications and provide robust educational and social support for immigrant youths. Effective integration programs can help tap into the full potential of immigrant populations, reducing underemployment and preventing the marginalization that leads to illegal activities. Host countries can mitigate negative sentiments and enhance social cohesion by fostering an inclusive environment and ensuring that immigrants can contribute meaningfully to the economy and society.

In addition, many immigrant youths face significant barriers to education and integration into society. Without access to proper educational opportunities and support systems, these young individuals often find themselves marginalized and disconnected from the mainstream community. This marginalization can push some towards illegal activities and gang involvement as they search for a sense of belonging and purpose. According to various studies, such as those conducted by the Migration Policy Institute, this trend contributes to increased crime rates and social issues within host countries, exacerbating anti-immigrant sentiments among the native population.

In light of these challenges, host countries must develop comprehensive integration policies that promote social cohesion while respecting immigrants' cultural identities. Initiatives such as language and vocational training, legal support, and community engagement programs can facilitate smoother transitions. For example, Canada's settlement services provide immigrants with language training, employment services, and community connections, helping them integrate more effectively into Canadian society.

Ultimately, creating an inclusive environment where immigrants can thrive benefits both the individuals and the broader society. By addressing the systemic barriers to integration and fostering a more inclusive approach, host countries can harness the full potential of their immigrant populations, leading to more diverse, vibrant, and prosperous communities.

Sometimes, the countries that immigrants are leaving employ controversial and coercive strategies to discourage host nations from accepting their citizens. One notable example occurred during the Mariel boatlift in 1980, when Cuban leader Fidel Castro opened the country's prisons and mental health facilities, allowing criminals and other institutionalized individuals to leave for the United States. This move was a deliberate attempt to burden the host country, in this case, the United States, with individuals who might cause social and economic strain.

Approximately 125,000 Cubans fled to the U.S. during the Mariel boatlift, seeking refuge and a better life. However, amidst the genuine asylum seekers and families hoping to reunite with their relatives in the U.S., Castro included a significant number of inmates from prisons and patients from mental institutions. This tactic aimed to disrupt the host nation's willingness to accept immigrants by introducing individuals who could potentially be seen as a threat to public safety and social stability.

Another historical example can be found during the Vietnamese boat people crisis following the Vietnam War. In the late 1970s and early 1980s, the Vietnamese government allowed and even encouraged certain segments of their population to flee by sea. This mass exodus included not only those persecuted by the communist regime but also individuals who were undesirable or problematic for the government. Neighboring countries in Southeast Asia, such as Malaysia and Thailand, were overwhelmed by the influx of refugees, which included a mix of genuine asylum seekers and those sent by the Vietnamese government to offload internal pressures.

In the early 2000s, Libya under Muammar Gaddafi also used migration as a political tool. Gaddafi threatened to flood Europe with African migrants unless the European Union increased financial aid and support to Libya. This strategy aimed to exert pressure on European nations by using the threat of uncontrolled migration as leverage in diplomatic negotiations.

There have been documented instances and persistent concerns about ISIS (the Islamic State of Iraq and Syria), a terrorist organization exploiting the refugee crisis to infiltrate operatives into Europe and the United States. Intelligence agencies have pointed to the 2015 Paris attacks as a case where this tactic was employed. Several of the terrorists involved in these attacks, which resulted in the deaths of 130 people, entered Europe posing as refugees by using fake Syrian passports. The attackers crossed through Greece as part of the broader wave of asylum seekers fleeing the Syrian civil war. This incident, along with subsequent warnings from European and American security agencies, underscores the complex security challenges host countries face.

These incidents underscore the complex and often manipulative nature of mass migrations orchestrated by governments for political ends. They highlight the necessity for comprehensive and nuanced immigration policies that can effectively distinguish between genuine refugees and those included in these movements for coercive reasons. Host countries must balance humanitarian obligations with ensuring public safety and social cohesion. Effective screening processes, support systems for integration, and international cooperation are essential to managing these challenges.

By understanding and addressing the underlying political motivations behind such migration strategies, host nations can better prepare for and respond to these complex scenarios. This ensures that they provide refuge to those in genuine need while maintaining their social and economic stability. Effective integration programs, recognition of foreign qualifications, and support services can help mitigate the negative impacts on infrastructure and the job market while enabling immigrants to contribute positively to their new communities.

Indeed, countries that welcome immigrants often reap significant benefits from the influx of new residents. Immigrants bring diverse skills and experiences, contributing to the host country's workforce in many vital sectors. Skilled and educated immigrants often fill gaps in professional fields such as technology, healthcare, and engineering, with a high demand for specialized knowledge. Meanwhile, blue-collar workers play an essential role in industries like construction, agriculture, and manufacturing, which are crucial for the economy but are often understaffed.

As the world population declines in many developed

countries, immigrants can play a crucial role in supplementing the workforce. These nations, facing aging populations and lower birth rates, often need additional labor to sustain economic growth and support social welfare systems. Immigrants bring vital skills and new perspectives that can help invigorate these aging workforces, contribute to innovation, and fill gaps in labor markets across various sectors. Furthermore, their integration into the workforce can lead to cultural enrichment and enhanced diversity, benefiting the broader society.

The contribution of immigrants extends beyond filling labor shortages. They also bring entrepreneurial spirit, innovative perspectives, and cultural diversity that can lead to new businesses and stimulate economic growth. Additionally, the cultural enrichment that accompanies immigration enhances the social fabric of the host country, promoting a more global and inclusive society. Thus, the impact of immigrants is profound and multifaceted, benefiting the economy, enriching the culture, and adding vitality to the community.

While immigrants need to cherish and maintain their own cultural, language, religious, and traditional practices as a vital part of their identity, integrating into and respecting the culture of their new home is equally crucial. This respect and willingness to adapt facilitate smoother transitions into the new community, fostering mutual understanding and respect among diverse populations.

Adapting to the local customs and legal frameworks helps newcomers build a sense of belonging and strengthens social cohesion within the community. This integration process often involves learning the local language, understanding the social norms, and participating in community and civic activities, which can enhance an immigrant's role in their new society. Simultaneously, host countries that encourage and celebrate cultural diversity while promoting inclusive policies can create a welcoming environment that values new and existing traditions. This symbiotic relationship benefits everyone by creating a more harmonious, vibrant, and resilient society.

When immigrants move to a new country, they need to find a balance between preserving their own cultural heritage and embracing the culture of their new home. Respecting the host country's existing cultural norms and values is essential. Attempting to impose one's own cultural practices on the local population can be perceived as disrespectful and may lead to tension and misunderstandings within the community.

Integration involves a reciprocal respect for diversity, where immigrants and native residents acknowledge and appreciate each other's cultural differences without imposing their own beliefs and practices. Effective integration encourages immigrants to contribute positively to the community while adapting to and respecting the local culture. This process enriches the host society and supports a cohesive and inclusive environment where diverse cultures are celebrated and mutual respect is upheld.

Navigating the complex issues surrounding immigration and historical context requires a nuanced understanding. Indeed, while the history of colonization has left profound and long-lasting effects on many nations and their migration patterns, using it as a justification for immigration policies can be contentious. Historical grievances are significant and inform the contemporary socio-political climate, yet they don't always provide clear directives for current policymaking.

Each country faces unique challenges in the modern context and must address its current economic, social, and environmental needs. It is crucial that all residents, both native-born and immigrant, contribute to their society to the best of their abilities. This contribution fosters a mutually beneficial relationship, helping to build a cohesive community and a robust national economy.

Furthermore, immigration policies need to be fair and considerate, considering the nation's needs and the rights and well-being of immigrants. Creating a supportive environment where immigrants can successfully integrate and contribute will lead to greater societal benefits, including cultural enrichment and economic growth. This approach requires moving beyond historical grievances to address the realities of today's globalized world, where cooperation, respect, and mutual understanding are vital to achieving societal harmony and progress.

Global migration dynamics are now shaped by a complex array of factors, including geopolitical tensions, religious differences, social injustices, climate change, wars, and political instability. As these pressures persist or escalate, migration will likely increase, presenting substantial challenges and opportunities for host countries. Proper planning, resource allocation, and policymaking are necessary to ensure that the influx of immigrants does not overwhelm local systems. This includes providing adequate infrastructure, healthcare, education, and employment opportunities.

For effective integration, the process must be mutual. Immigrants should try to understand, respect, and adapt to their new countries' legal frameworks, cultural norms, and social values. This helps build mutual respect and eases their incorporation into the community. Conversely, host societies need to be open and inclusive, recognizing the potential benefits of a diverse population. Policies that encourage participation in the local economy and community activities can help leverage the unique contributions of immigrants.

Constructive integration strategies can mitigate potential conflicts and facilitate a smoother transition for immigrants, helping them become active, contributing members of their new communities. This balanced approach not only supports the well-being of the immigrants but also enhances the host countries' social, cultural, and economic fabric. As the world moves forward, fostering dialogue, understanding, and cooperation between all parties will be critical to effectively addressing global migration's challenges.

It is commonly believed that a person belongs to two families: the one of their birth and the one they choose. This concept can also be extended to one's home country. Many individuals find themselves connected to the country of their birth, with its deep-rooted traditions and cultural heritage, and the country they choose to make their new home, where they build a future and create new bonds.

This duality reflects the complex nature of identity and belonging, where people can cherish their origins while embracing new experiences and opportunities. For immigrants, this means maintaining a connection to their cultural roots while integrating into the fabric of their adopted country, creating a rich tapestry of diverse influences and perspectives.

Many immigrants who successfully resettle feel lucky to have found a country they can call home. These individuals often discover that their adopted nations provide them with the resources needed to succeed—opportunities they might not have found in their native countries under different circumstances. This striking contrast makes many immigrants value the chances their new countries provide. Their appreciation extends to personal achievements and the overall benefits their presence brings to these nations. In these welcoming environments, they can thrive and establish fulfilling lives, contributing positively to their new homes' societal and economic fabric.

The global political landscape is increasingly shifting towards right-wing nationalist governments that are adopting stricter anti-immigrant policies. These governments are implementing new regulations to prevent immigrants from entering their countries or deporting those already within their borders. This trend is evident in various countries across Europe, North America, and other regions, where there is growing resistance to immigration fueled by economic concerns, cultural tensions, and security issues.

In Europe, countries like Hungary and Poland have implemented strict immigration policies and fortified their borders. Under Prime Minister Viktor Orbán, Hungary has built border fences and refused to accept EU migrant quotas. Similarly, Poland has taken a firm stance against accepting large numbers of refugees and migrants.

In the United States, the Trump administration (2017-2021)

saw a significant tightening of immigration policies, including the implementation of a travel ban targeting several predominantly Muslim countries and efforts to build a wall along the U.S.-Mexico border. These measures were aimed at curbing illegal immigration and addressing national security concerns.

The United Kingdom's Brexit campaign was partly driven by a desire to regain control over immigration policies. Following Brexit, the UK has implemented a points-based immigration system to limit the number of low-skilled workers entering the country, reflecting a broader desire to control immigration more tightly.

This shift towards stricter immigration policies reflects a broader trend of increasing nationalism and protectionism as these governments respond to their constituents' concerns about economic security, cultural identity, and national sovereignty.

Despite these stringent measures, desperate people seek refuge and better opportunities, often risking their lives. As legal pathways become more restricted, illegal trafficking networks are thriving. Smugglers are capitalizing on the desperation of migrants by charging exorbitant fees and resorting to increasingly dangerous methods to transport them across borders. This has led to a rise in perilous journeys, with many migrants facing life-threatening conditions, exploitation, and abuse along the way.

For instance, in recent years, there have been numerous

reports of overcrowded boats capsizing in the Mediterranean Sea, resulting in tragic loss of life. Migrants have also been found in inhumane conditions in hidden compartments of vehicles or trekking through harsh terrains without adequate supplies. The tightening of immigration policies has inadvertently contributed to the growth of these illicit operations, making the plight of refugees and migrants even direr and underscoring the need for comprehensive, humane solutions to address the complex issues of global migration.

The influx of immigrants is not just a problem for the United States and Europe; many other countries worldwide are also facing significant challenges related to immigration.

The situation is particularly dire in Africa. The continent is experiencing significant migration pressures due to conflict, economic instability, and environmental challenges. Countries like Nigeria, South Sudan, and the Democratic Republic of the Congo have seen large numbers of their populations displaced due to internal conflicts and violence. These internally displaced people often seek refuge in neighboring countries, further straining regional resources.

North African countries, such as Libya and Tunisia, have become key transit points for migrants attempting to reach Europe. These nations are dealing with the dual pressures of managing their own economic and social challenges while accommodating large numbers of migrants and refugees. The journey through North Africa to Europe is perilous, often involving human trafficking networks and dangerous sea crossings.

Malaysia and Thailand have become major destinations for migrants and refugees from Myanmar, particularly the Rohingya minority fleeing persecution. These countries face the complex task of managing large refugee populations while dealing with their own economic and social pressures.

Conversely, India sees significant migration from neighboring countries such as Bangladesh and Nepal, driven by economic opportunities and climate-induced displacement. The influx puts additional pressure on India's already strained resources and infrastructure, creating tensions and necessitating robust immigration policies and support systems.

As the situation in Afghanistan remains unstable, with ongoing conflict and economic hardship, many Afghans are fleeing to neighboring countries. In Turkey, the government has had to balance its domestic concerns with the needs of the large refugee population, which includes not only Afghans but also Syrians and others fleeing conflict and persecution. The country has implemented various policies to manage this influx, but the strain on resources and infrastructure is palpable. Iran, similarly, hosts a significant number of Afghan refugees. The influx has pressured Iran's economy and social services, especially in border regions.

Pakistan is also significantly impacted by the influx of Afghan refugees. Sharing a long and porous border with Afghanistan, Pakistan has been a primary destination for Afghan refugees for decades. As of 2021, Pakistan hosts nearly 3 million Afghan refugees, making it one of the largest refugee-hosting countries in the world. The continuous influx has strained Pakistan's resources, particularly in terms of healthcare, education, and housing in the border regions. The economic burden is substantial, and the social services in refugee-hosting areas are under significant stress. Additionally, the presence of a large refugee population has led to complex security concerns and political tensions within the country.

Mass immigration is likely to worsen before it improves. In addition to wars and the pursuit of better opportunities, the accelerating effects of climate change are expected to significantly increase the rate of mass immigration, making it a pressing global issue. Rising sea levels, extreme weather events, and the degradation of arable land will force millions to leave their homes in search of safer and more stable environments. This inevitable surge in climate refugees will place unprecedented demands on host countries, particularly well-off ones.

Several regions worldwide are expected to see increased migration due to the accelerating effects of climate change. South Asia, particularly India and Bangladesh, faces significant risks from rising sea levels and extreme weather events. The World Bank estimates that by 2050, climate change could force 13.3 million people to migrate within Bangladesh alone.

In Sub-Saharan Africa, the Sahel region is experiencing severe desertification, rendering vast land areas uninhabitable. This environmental degradation forces populations to migrate in search of arable land and water sources, creating significant migration flows within and across national borders. The United Nations estimates this could displace up to 86 million people by 2050. According to the UN, East Africa is also affected, with frequent droughts and floods disrupting agriculture and livelihoods, pushing people to migrate to more stable regions. In North Africa, countries like Egypt, Tunisia, and Libya are grappling with severe water scarcity and land degradation, with the Nile Delta in Egypt being particularly vulnerable to sea-level rise.

The Middle East is also at high risk, with countries such as Syria, Iran, and Iraq expected to experience more intense and frequent heatwaves and droughts, exacerbating existing conflicts and increasing displacement.

Pacific Island nations, including Kiribati, Tuvalu, and the

Maldives, face the existential threat of rising sea levels, which could render many of these islands uninhabitable by the end of the century.

In Latin America, Central American countries like Honduras, Guatemala, and El Salvador are confronting severe droughts and extreme weather events, potentially displacing 17 million people within the region by 2050, according to the World Bank.

Similarly, in Southeast Asia, areas like the Mekong Delta in Vietnam and low-lying regions in Indonesia, including Jakarta, are highly vulnerable to flooding and sea-level rise, with tens of millions of people potentially displaced by 2050, as estimated by the Asian Development Bank.

These nations must develop and implement comprehensive policies to address this challenge. Such policies should include robust support systems for integration, recognition of foreign qualifications, and the provision of adequate infrastructure and resources. By acting proactively, well-off countries can mitigate the potential strain on their social and economic systems while ensuring humane and just treatment for those displaced by climate change. Addressing this issue with foresight and compassion is crucial for fostering global stability and resilience in an uncertain future.

These regions highlight the urgent need for global cooperation and robust policy measures to address climate-induced migration. Preparing for these scenarios involves investing in climate resilience, developing sustainable livelihoods, and creating legal frameworks to protect and support climate migrants. The challenges ahead are immense, but with proactive and coordinated efforts, the international community can mitigate the impacts of climate-induced migration and support affected populations.

Historical Cycles: Learning from the Past to Navigate the Future

"Those who cannot remember the past are condemned to repeat it."- George Santayana

Amidst the clinking of glasses and the lively exchange of stories at a spirited dinner gathering, compelling icebreaker questions often emerge to captivate the imaginations of all present: "If you could invite a person from any time to this event, who would it be and why?" or, "If you had the chance, would you travel back in history or leap forward into the future? And why?" These simple questions open a gateway to fascinating debates about time, personal values, and the myriad possibilities of each choice.

Such questions serve as more than just conversation starters; they ignite deep reflections and discussions about the nature of our curiosity and the impact of historical and future events on our lives. Revisiting the past or exploring the future taps into our desires to understand our roots, explore other historical eras, or foresee the unknown. It prompts considerations of the lessons we can learn from history versus the advancements and challenges we might encounter in the future.

"If you had the chance, would you travel back in history or

leap forward into the future? And why?" This question, in particular, delves deep into our motivations and desires, offering a rich avenue for discussion. It compels us to weigh the value of historical understanding against the allure of future possibilities, sparking conversations about what truly shapes our perspectives and dreams.

While I delve into history in this section and explore science and science fiction in the next, my curiosity often leans towards journeying into the future to witness firsthand humanity's progression and advancements. The allure of the future lies in its mysteries and the potential to experience the culmination of today's technological and societal evolutions. There is an undeniable fascination with seeing how current innovations will shape our world, understanding the advancements in science and technology, and experiencing potential societal changes.

Conversely, the past offers a compelling invitation to walk through history and witness the events and figures shaping our world. Exploring history provides a unique opportunity to understand the origins of our current societies, the evolution of cultures, and the pivotal moments that have influenced our present. Observing historical events as they happened and meeting influential figures from different eras adds depth to our understanding of humanity's journey.

Both directions in time offer their own unique fascinations

and insights. While the future promises innovation and new experiences, the past offers rich lessons and context for understanding how we arrived at our present state. Therefore, my exploration will cover both realms, appreciating the lessons of history and the possibilities of the future.

This dual interest enriches my perspective, allowing me to appreciate the lessons of the past while eagerly anticipating the innovations the future might bring. Understanding history provides context for our present and informs our future, while science and science fiction fuel our imaginations and expand our visions of what is possible. Together, these topics interlace a rich mosaic of knowledge and inspiration, shaping our understanding of the world and our place within it.

Reading historical books has offered me profound insights into the patterns and cycles of human behavior, illustrating the saying that history often repeats itself. This perspective becomes particularly intriguing when examining pivotal moments like revolutions and wars where parallels emerge across different cultures and eras.

When delving into history books and exploring events such as revolutions, it becomes evident that despite varying cultural and political contexts, specific patterns recur, often leading to significant upheavals.

We can discern common areas that contributed to revolutionary conditions in each by examining the Tsarist era in Russia, pre-revolutionary Cuba, and Iran before the Islamic Revolution. In the shadows of the 20th century, a series of revolutions reshaped the political landscapes of Russia, Cuba, and Iran. Each was driven by a complex weave of social, economic, and ideological forces that echo through the annals of history.

Each of these societies was under the thumb of autocratic rulers who wielded power without restraint and curtailed political freedoms. Tsar Nicholas II of Russia, Fulgencio Batista of Cuba, and Shah Mohammad Reza Pahlavi of Iran all governed with a heavy hand, suppressing dissent. This suppression created an undercurrent of widespread dissatisfaction, setting the stage for the revolutionary fervor that would eventually lead to the downfall of these regimes.

During the political oppression, stark economic disparities were blatantly apparent. In Tsarist Russia, the contrast between the wealthy lives of a few and the dire poverty faced by the masses was stark. Similar scenes played out in Cuba and Iran, where corruption and policies favoring the elite further deepened economic inequalities. This was particularly inflammatory in Iran despite the country's considerable oil wealth, as the financial benefits seemed disproportionately skewed, fueling widespread public discontent and anger.

As these regions each pushed toward modernization, often influenced by the West, the societal impacts were profound. Tsarist Russia's industrial efforts, Batista's Cuba with its strong American business connections, and the Shah of Iran's push for Western-style modernization policies all led to significant cultural clashes. Traditional segments of these societies felt increasingly alienated and marginalized, perceiving these changes as threats to their way of life.

Revolutionary ideologies took root and flourished during this backdrop of autocracy and inequality. In Russia, Marxist ideas about class struggle resonated deeply with the oppressed working classes. In Cuba and Iran, though the ideologies varied, the revolutions were predominantly fueled by nationalism and anti-imperialism, coupled with a robust demand for social justice. These ideologies mobilized the masses and provided a structured framework for revolutionary action, giving people the motivation and the means to challenge their rulers.

In these transformative times, intellectuals and the military played critical roles. In Russia, intellectuals spread anti-tsarist sentiments, laying the ideological groundwork for revolution. In Cuba and Iran, the situation reached a tipping point when key military figures aligned themselves with revolutionary forces, a crucial element for the success of these movements.

Reflecting on these historical upheavals reveals patterns and parallels with other significant revolutions around the globe, such as the French Revolution, the Chinese Revolution, and the Mexican Revolution. These movements also grappled with autocratic governance, stark economic disparities, and the influential roles of revolutionary ideologies and key societal figures. These elements combined catalyze profound change in each case, reshaping nations and their histories.

As we delve into these narratives, it's clear that while the context and characters may differ, the stories of revolution are woven from similar threads—despotism, disparity, and the powerful human desire for freedom and fairness. These revolutions remind us that when governance fails to reflect the will and welfare of the people, the seeds of change find fertile ground in the hearts of the oppressed, eventually growing into movements that can alter the courses of nations.

These revolutions underscore the critical roles played by socioeconomic inequalities, autocratic governance, the clash between traditional values and modernization, and the spread of revolutionary ideologies. While unique in its cultural and historical context, each revolution shows how similar pressures can lead to significant social and political transformations across different regions and epochs. This comparative analysis enhances our understanding of how such conditions may still be relevant in analyzing worldwide socio-political developments.

Understanding these historical patterns provides a window into the past and a lens through which current events can be viewed. Recognizing the signs of societal unrest, economic disparity, and the effects of rapid modernization can help analyze contemporary political situations. Moreover, studying these histories encourages a deeper understanding of how structural inequalities, if unaddressed, can lead to significant societal upheavals. This kind of historical insight is invaluable for scholars, policymakers, and anyone interested in the dynamics of societal change.

Moreover, by understanding past events, successes, and failures, leaders can make more informed decisions, avoid previous mistakes, and navigate challenges more effectively. Ignoring history often leads to repeating the same errors, hindering progress and development.

Considering these common elements can provide valuable lessons for today, as they highlight the potential consequences of unchecked autocratic power, economic inequality, forced modernization, and the power of ideology. These historical insights can help us anticipate and mitigate similar conditions in contemporary contexts, illustrating the profound impact of historical knowledge in shaping our understanding of past and future events.

As I delve deeper into historical texts, I appreciate their

immense value in recounting past events and understanding potential future scenarios. History often shows repetitive patterns and conditions that, under similar circumstances, might lead to comparable outcomes in different times or places. To illustrate, we can draw parallels between the corruption seen in post-revolution Iran and post-communist Russia by examining their sociopolitical and economic climates after systemic changes.

Following the 1979 Islamic Revolution, Iran transformed from a monarchy under Shah Mohammad Reza Pahlavi to an Islamic Republic under Ayatollah Khomeini. This shift led to the establishment of a theocratic regime that centralized religious and political authority, spurring allegations of corruption, particularly concerning economic disparities and resource control. Entities like the Revolutionary Guards (IRGC) extended their influence into the construction, telecommunications, and energy sectors, raising concerns about corruption and cronyism.

In contrast, after the Soviet Union dissolved in 1991, Russia transitioned from a centrally planned economy to a market-oriented one under Boris Yeltsin. This chaotic transition was marked by widespread corruption. Rapid privatization allowed minor business oligarchs to amass significant wealth by acquiring state assets at undervalued prices, a period often referred to as the "wild 90s." This era was characterized by significant economic inequality, lax regulatory oversight, and pervasive corruption at various levels of government and business.

Both countries saw a centralization of power that facilitated corruption. In Iran, power consolidated within the theocratic elite, while in Russia, the political elite and emerging oligarchs benefited from the absence of effective governance during the transition. Economic reforms in both nations led to substantial disparities; in Iran, the state controlled many economic sectors, offering preferential treatment to those connected to the regime, whereas, in Russia, rapid privatization fostered a new class of wealthy individuals. At the same time, the general populace often endured economic hardships. Additionally, the IRGC in Iran and the security apparatus in Russia both played significant roles in consolidating power for the ruling elites. They benefited from new economic opportunities, exerting considerable influence on national policies.

While Iran and Russia's specific historical and cultural contexts differ markedly, both countries exhibit patterns of corruption. Power and wealth become concentrated in the hands of a few, often at the expense of the general populace. This has led to ongoing challenges in establishing transparent and accountable governance systems.

On a personal note, I have witnessed life during the Shah's rule and experienced the aftermath of the 1979 revolution. While the Shah was indeed a dictator, he aimed to modernize the country, fighting against deeply rooted traditions to push Iran forward. His efforts included significant infrastructural development, educational reforms, and attempts to secularize the nation. Despite his autocratic methods, some policies were geared towards modernization and economic progress. However, the new regime that came into power after the revolution has proven far more oppressive. The current rulers use their power not to advance the nation but to spread hatred both within Iran and beyond its borders. Their focus has been on maintaining a strict theocratic rule, suppressing dissent even more brutally than the Shah, and fostering an environment of fear and intolerance. The hope for a better future that fueled the revolution has been replaced by a regime that prioritizes ideological conformity over the welfare and progress of its people.

Indeed, the patterns observed in the historical events surrounding the Iranian Revolution are not isolated examples; similar dynamics can be found throughout other historical events, including wars. This repetition underscores a broader historical theme: certain structural factors, such as economic disparities, political unrest, and social inequalities, often lead to similar outcomes across different contexts and eras.

Similarly, the American and French revolutions share commonalities with Iran's in their origins—stemming from economic grievances, demands for greater representation, and a push against an out-of-touch ruling elite.

This pattern recognition helps us understand specific events and the underlying forces that drive history. By studying these repetitions, we can better anticipate future challenges and, with careful planning and reform, steer toward more peaceful and equitable resolutions. It emphasizes the importance of learning from history to recognize early warning signs and potentially mitigate similar conflicts in the future.

Historical analysis offers crucial insights into effective decision-making by highlighting the outcomes of past policies. This knowledge allows leaders and policymakers to learn from previous successes and avoid past mistakes, underscoring the importance of historical knowledge in predicting and addressing future issues.

Moreover, it provides a deep understanding of human behavior in various situations, including crisis responses, governance, and economic changes. This understanding is pivotal for forecasting how individuals and societies respond to analogous circumstances today.

By examining the historical trajectories of right and left ideologies, we can better appreciate the complexities and ongoing developments that shape governmental and societal priorities today. Understanding the histories of these movements provides crucial context for current political debates and policies in Europe and the U.S.

The political spectrums of right and left have long shaped the government dynamics of Europe and the U.S., reflecting broader social, economic, and ideological trends. The origins of these terms trace back to the French Revolution, where deputies in the National Assembly sat according to their allegiances—supporters of the king on the right and supporters of the revolution on the left. This distinction set the stage for centuries of political evolution, with Europe's right-wing generally advocating for conservative values and hierarchical social order and the left-wing pushing for progressive reforms and expanded civil liberties.

In the United States, although the political spectrum is similarly divided into conservative (right) and liberal (left) ideologies, it features distinct characteristics shaped by a two-party system dominated by Republicans and Democrats. Historical events like the Civil War, the Great Depression, and the civil rights movement have notably influenced shifts in these ideologies.

Both European and American political landscapes often shift in response to economic crises. For instance, the Great Depression spurred the New Deal in the U.S., led by left-leaning Democrats, akin to the economic instabilities in post-World War I Germany that catalyzed significant political shifts toward both extremes of the spectrum.

The drive for social reforms has been a hallmark of the left in both regions. In Europe, 19th and 20th-century labor movements and, in the U.S., the civil rights movement have been pivotal in advocating for workers' rights, racial equality, and welfare support, resulting in substantial legislative and societal changes.

The influence of monarchical versus republican traditions also differentiates European and American politics. Due to Europe's monarchical history, Europe's right-wing movements have often been associated with preserving monarchy and aristocracy. In contrast, the U.S., founded on principles of republicanism and anti-monarchical sentiment, aligns its right-wing ideologies more with free market principles and individual liberties.

Additionally, Europe has a more robust tradition of formally organized socialist and communist parties, such as Germany's SPD or France's PCF, which have played significant roles in shaping political agendas. In contrast, in the U.S., socialist and communist ideologies have been less mainstream and often stigmatized, especially during the Cold War, reflecting different cultural and historical influences on political ideology in the two regions.

The globalism movement of the late 1900s had profound impacts on the United States, Europe, and countries worldwide, reshaping economic landscapes, cultural dynamics, and political alliances.

In the United States, the push towards neoliberal economic

policies continued under Presidents Reagan, Bush, and Clinton, emphasizing deregulation, privatization, and reduced government spending on social services. These changes promoted a more market-oriented economy, which, while stimulating economic growth and technological innovation, also widened income inequality and reduced the welfare safety net. On a cultural level, the U.S. emerged as a dominant force in global media, entertainment, and consumer culture, exporting its values and lifestyle through movies, music, and television, influencing global culture.

Europe experienced similar transformations under leaders like Margaret Thatcher in the UK and later leaders across the continent, emphasizing free market principles that were replicated in various forms across Europe. The European Union, which grew from the European Community in the 1990s, furthered economic cooperation and began to form a more integrated single market. This integration directly manifested globalist ideas, promoting the free movement of goods, services, people, and capital across borders. The fall of the Berlin Wall and the subsequent easing of Cold War tensions also opened Eastern Europe to influences from the West. They accelerated the integration of the continent both economically and politically.

In other parts of the world, the impacts of globalism were mixed. Many Asian countries, particularly China and India, began to open their economies to the world in the 1980s and 1990s, which led to significant economic growth and integration into the global economy. These changes, however, also brought challenges such as environmental damage, social displacement, and cultural upheavals. Latin America, influenced heavily by the Washington Consensus, adopted similar economic policies, which, in some cases, led to short-term economic gains and significant social and economic instability, often exacerbating issues of debt and inequality.

Furthermore, globalism influenced the political structures and economic policies in Africa and the Middle East, where structural adjustment programs were implemented. These programs, guided by international financial institutions, aimed at economic liberalization and reducing government deficits but often resulted in social unrest and a decrease in public services, impacting the socioeconomic fabric of these regions.

The globalism movement of the late 1900s, therefore, had far-reaching effects across the globe, fundamentally altering economic policies, cultural exchanges, and political alliances. While it drove economic integration and the spread of technology and media, it also presented challenges that continue to be addressed in subsequent decades. The legacy of this era is a more interconnected world that faces complex challenges requiring cooperative global responses.

The rapid pace of cultural and demographic changes fueled by immigration and the global movement of people contributed to social instability. In many European countries, increasing numbers of immigrants from the Middle East, Africa, and Eastern Europe during the late 1990s and early 2000s led to cultural tensions and a perceived threat to national identity among some population segments. Economic uncertainties often exacerbated these sentiments. They were seized upon by nationalist political parties, which began to gain traction by advocating for stricter immigration controls and the preservation of traditional cultural values.

Nationalism has long been a powerful force in shaping world history, evident in many pivotal events across different eras. In the 19th century, nationalist sentiments were crucial in the unification of Germany and Italy, where shared language, culture, and history helped forge strong national identities. This unity was instrumental in merging various independent states into cohesive nations.

During World War I and II, nationalism significantly influenced the global landscape. It fueled nationalistic fervor that mobilized populations and justified extensive military expansions, often under the guise of national pride and protection. This intense national pride sometimes escalated into aggressive foreign policies and conflicts.

The financial crises of the late 2000s further undermined

faith in global economic policies. The 2008 global financial crisis, in particular, had devastating effects worldwide, severely impacting economies and exposing the vulnerabilities of an interconnected global financial system. The crisis led to significant public discontent with the status quo, which nationalist politicians used to their advantage, criticizing globalist policies for favoring the elite at the expense of the average citizen.

As a result, the early 2000s witnessed a resurgence of nationalism in many parts of the world, marked by a growing skepticism of globalization and a reassertion of national sovereignty. Therefore, in recent years, there has been a noticeable resurgence of nationalist movements across the globe, marked by a strong emphasis on national sovereignty, stringent immigration policies, and often a critical perspective on globalization and international institutions. Various economic, social, and political factors have driven this rise, such as economic uncertainty, cultural fears, and a backlash against the perceived overreach of supranational entities like the European Union.

In the United States, Donald Trump's 2016 election campaign was heavily laden with nationalist rhetoric, encapsulated by his "America First" slogan. His presidency focused on tightening immigration policies, renegotiating trade agreements, and reevaluating U.S. participation in international accords. Notable actions included withdrawing from the Paris Climate Accord, which aimed to combat global climate change, and the Trans-Pacific Partnership (TPP), a significant trade agreement to strengthen economic ties among Pacific Rim countries. Additionally, his administration implemented travel bans on several predominantly Muslim countries and imposed tariffs on imports from China, aiming to reduce the trade deficit and protect American industries.

Similarly, nationalism played a pivotal role in the United Kingdom's Brexit movement, which led to the decision to leave the European Union in 2016. Brexit advocates pushed for the reclamation of legislative and border control, arguing that this would enable better immigration management and more autonomous economic policies.

Vladimir Putin's actions towards Russia's neighbors, especially Ukraine, are deeply rooted in nationalism and strategic geopolitical interests. The annexation of Crimea in 2014 and the ongoing support for separatists in Eastern Ukraine are key examples framed by Putin as measures to protect ethnic Russians and reclaim historically Russian territories. His 2022 full-scale invasion of Ukraine was justified with similar narratives of defending Russian speakers and resisting NATO expansion, reflecting a broader strategy to assert Russia's influence and security concerns. State-controlled media in Russia amplifies this nationalist rhetoric, portraying Russia as besieged by external threats, thereby rallying domestic support for Putin's policies. This approach illustrates how

Putin uses historical grievances and nationalism to legitimize his regional ambitions.

Right-wing and Euroskeptic parties made significant gains in the 2024 European Parliament elections. This shift is attributed to various factors, including a decline in support for mainstream political parties and an increase in nationalist and populist sentiments across Europe. Such trends reflect broader public discontent with current political leadership and policies, particularly regarding immigration and national sovereignty.

In countries like Italy, Sweden, and Finland, far-right parties have gained governmental roles, reflecting a growing acceptance of these groups in national politics. This acceptance is also influenced by the charismatic leadership of figures like Giorgia Meloni in Italy, who has significantly impacted the broader European political landscape, particularly concerning policies on migration and climate.

The far-right National Rally (RN) 's victory in France during the 2024 elections had significant implications for the country and Europe. Under the leadership of Jordan Bardella and Marine Le Pen, the RN achieved a remarkable 31.5% of the vote in the European Parliament elections, positioning it as a formidable political force.

In reaction to these results, President Emmanuel Macron dissolved the National Assembly and called for snap elections on

June 30, 2024. This move was part of his strategy to counter the growing influence of the far right and regain political stability in France.

These developments have sparked widespread debate and concern, highlighting the increasing polarization and challenges traditional political structures face in dealing with the rise of far-right movements. Macron's actions and the RN's successes illustrate the dynamic and sometimes volatile nature of French and European politics in 2024.

The far-right's success in France marks a dramatic shift in the political landscape, reflecting deep public dissatisfaction with the current government. The National Rally (RN)'s platform, which includes stringent anti-immigration policies and a focus on national preference, challenges France's traditional centrist and leftist policies. If the RN continues to gain ground, it could significantly influence France's domestic and foreign policies, potentially leading to stricter immigration controls and reevaluating France's role in the European Union.

In the second round of the 2024 French legislative elections, left-wing parties formed an alliance known as the New Popular Ecological and Social Union (NUPES). This coalition included the Socialists, Greens, Communists, and the far-left France Insoumise. Their collaboration was pivotal in preventing the far-right National

Rally (RN) from securing a decisive victory. By joining forces, these left-wing parties won enough seats to challenge President Emmanuel Macron's party, ultimately leading to a more balanced distribution of power in the French National Assembly. This alliance demonstrated the strategic importance of unity among left-leaning factions in countering the rise of far-right movements in French politics. Despite this, the far-right movement's influence remains significant and continues to shape the political discourse in France.

On a broader scale, the rise of the far-right in France mirrors a broader trend across Europe, where right-wing and far-right parties have made substantial gains in countries like Italy, Germany, and Hungary. This shift is likely to impact the European Parliament, as these parties collectively could become a significant force, influencing EU policies on immigration, climate change, and economic regulations. The European People's Party, despite being the largest single bloc, will need to navigate these new dynamics carefully to maintain stability and forge effective coalitions.

The implications for Europe are profound. A more substantial far-right presence could lead to more fragmented and polarized politics within the EU, challenging efforts to implement cohesive policies across member states. Issues such as climate policy, migration, and economic integration could become more contentious, potentially stalling progress and leading to increased tension among EU countries.

Additionally, the increasing influence of right-wing parties in the European Parliament is poised to steer policy in a more conservative direction, particularly concerning environmental regulations and immigration. This shift will likely weaken initiatives like the European Union Green Deal and enforce stricter immigration controls. Such changes significantly depart from previous globalist approaches, reflecting a broader trend toward nationalism and reevaluating policies that traditionally support open borders and international cooperation. The rise of right-wing parties is reshaping the EU's political dynamics, signaling a potentially more fragmented and nationalist future for the region.

In India, Prime Minister Narendra Modi's tenure has been characterized by a surge in Hindu nationalism, with government policies and discourse frequently highlighting Hindu identity and values as fundamental to Indian society. This has been evident in several legislative actions, most notably the controversial revocation of Article 370 in Kashmir.

Meanwhile, Brazil witnessed the rise of Jair Bolsonaro, elected in 2018 on a platform that championed traditional values, prioritized Brazilian interests in trade and environmental issues, and promoted stringent measures against crime and corruption. Each case demonstrates how nationalism shapes political landscapes worldwide, responding to local contexts and global interactions.

The mid-20th century also witnessed a powerful wave of nationalism during the decolonization movements in Asia and Africa. Nations under colonial rule fought for independence, driven by a strong desire for self-rule and the preservation of their local traditions and governance. This period marked a significant reshaping of international relations and geopolitical boundaries as countries reclaimed their sovereignty and embarked on paths to self-determination.

While nationalism can reinforce community and cultural pride, it poses challenges, such as increased polarization and tension within and between nations. Understanding these dynamics requires looking at the specific national contexts that fuel these movements and the broader historical patterns of how nationalism has shaped global relations.

This view of recent nationalist movements, set against historical precedents, helps explain why these movements gained traction and what potential consequences might follow for international cooperation and domestic governance.

These insights are crucial; they teach us that history doesn't repeat itself arbitrarily. Instead, it does so because our basic human nature remains constant despite the evolution of societies and technologies. Understanding this can help us better anticipate future challenges and opportunities, recognizing that the drivers behind historical events are very much alive in today's world.

This perspective allows us to use history as a record of the past and as a guide that might inform our present decisions and strategies. It can help us manage conflicts, navigate societal changes, and foster better relationships in an ever-evolving world.

When you delve into history books and grasp how people have behaved across different eras, you realize that while times may change, people fundamentally do not. We continue to exhibit the same range of emotions—joy, love, fear, ego, anger—and these unchanging human characteristics often lead to the cyclical nature of history.

Throughout history, empires have often sown the seeds of their own destruction from within. Once a paragon of military might and administrative efficiency, the Roman Empire succumbed to internal decay marked by political corruption, economic instability, and overextension of its borders.

Similarly, the British Empire, which ruled over vast swathes of the globe, faced its downfall due to the unsustainable burden of maintaining such an extensive empire, coupled with rising nationalist movements and economic strains from two world wars.

The Ottoman Empire, too, crumbled under the weight of internal strife, bureaucratic inefficiencies, and the inability to modernize in the face of emerging European powers.

The Soviet Union, despite its formidable ideological and military presence, disintegrated due to economic stagnation, political repression, and the untenable costs of the arms race and Cold War confrontations.

These historical narratives highlight a common theme: empires often collapse not solely due to external pressures but because of their internal failures to adapt, govern effectively, and address systemic issues. The lessons from these past empires underscore the importance of sustainable governance, economic balance, and social cohesion in maintaining a stable and enduring nation.

Recent global government debt has reached unprecedented levels, with public debt totaling around $97 trillion in 2023. This surge, driven by economic crises, the COVID-19 pandemic, and extensive fiscal stimulus measures, presents significant global challenges to economic stability and growth. High debt levels strain national budgets, particularly in developing countries, diverting resources from critical areas such as healthcare and education. In many African nations, debt interest payments exceed investments in these essential sectors, impeding human development and economic progress. Additionally, the high debt burden raises borrowing costs, leading to a cycle of increased debt and economic strain. As interest rates rise, servicing debt becomes more expensive, reducing the fiscal space available for productive investments and social spending. This dynamic is particularly problematic in an environment of slow economic growth.

Excessive debt has significantly impacted nations, often leading to economic crises, social unrest, and political upheaval. The Great Depression of the 1930s is a notable example of how excessive debt played a critical role. The United States and many other countries experienced an economic boom during the 1920s, leading to high borrowing levels by individuals, businesses, and governments. When the stock market crashed in 1929, the debt-fueled economic expansion became a massive financial collapse. Banks failed, businesses went bankrupt, and millions lost their jobs. The economic downturn was exacerbated by deflation, which increased the real burden of debt. The Great Depression led to widespread poverty, social dislocation, and significant political changes, including the rise of protectionist policies and the eventual emergence of the New Deal in the United States.

In the 1980s, several Latin American countries faced severe economic difficulties due to excessive borrowing during the 1970s. Nations like Mexico, Brazil, and Argentina accumulated large amounts of debt from international lenders, primarily to finance development projects and boost economic growth. However, when global interest rates rose sharply in the early 1980s, these countries struggled to service their debt. Mexico's declaration of insolvency in 1982 marked the beginning of the Latin American debt crisis. The crisis led to a "lost decade" of economic stagnation, high inflation, and social instability across the region. Structural adjustment programs imposed by the International Monetary Fund (IMF) demanded austerity measures, which further deepened social hardships.

In the 2000s, characterized by hyperinflation, Zimbabwe's economic crisis also stemmed from unsustainable fiscal policies and excessive debt. The government's extensive land reform program, which involved the seizure and redistribution of commercial farmland, led to a collapse in agricultural production and a sharp decline in export revenues. The government resorted to printing money to finance its expenditures, leading to hyperinflation. At its peak in 2008, Zimbabwe's monthly inflation rate reached an astronomical 89.7 sextillion percent. The economic collapse caused widespread poverty, mass emigration, and a severe humanitarian crisis. The devaluation of the currency rendered savings worthless and disrupted everyday economic activities.

Greece's debt crisis in the early 2010s is a modern example of the devastating effects of excessive national debt. By 2009, Greece's public debt had reached 130% of GDP due to years of fiscal mismanagement, corruption, and uncontrolled spending. The global financial crisis of 2008 further exacerbated Greece's economic troubles. In 2010, Greece received a bailout from the European Union (EU) and the IMF, with strict austerity measures. These measures led to significant cuts in public spending, pensions, and wages, causing widespread protests and social unrest. The Greek economy contracted sharply, unemployment soared, and the country experienced a severe humanitarian crisis. Greece's debt crisis highlighted the vulnerabilities of the Eurozone and had ripple effects across global financial markets.

These historical examples demonstrate that excessive debt can lead to severe economic, social, and political consequences. High debt levels can make countries vulnerable to external shocks, such as changes in global interest rates or economic downturns, and constrain their ability to respond effectively to crises. Sustainable fiscal policies, effective debt management, and economic diversification are crucial to avoid the pitfalls of excessive debt.

For modern economies, including the United States, managing growing debt levels is essential to maintaining economic stability and ensuring a prosperous future. By learning from these historical precedents, nations can better navigate the complexities of debt management and economic policy, striving to create resilient and sustainable economies that can withstand the challenges of the global financial system.

The United States, as one of the largest economies, faces significant debt challenges. U.S. government debt is projected to rise to 133.9% of GDP by 2029, up from 122.1% in 2023. This growing debt burden has several implications. High levels of debt increase vulnerability to economic shocks. In a financial crisis or economic downturn, the ability to implement fiscal stimulus may be limited due to already high debt levels. As U.S. debt grows, so do the costs of servicing it. Higher interest rates needed to attract investors to U.S. Treasury bonds will increase the burden on the federal budget, potentially crowding out other essential expenditures. The Federal Reserve may face pressure to maintain low interest rates to keep borrowing costs manageable, conflicting with efforts to control inflation. This balancing act complicates monetary policy and can lead to prolonged economic instability. The U.S. debt affects global financial markets, as U.S. Treasury bonds are a benchmark for global interest rates. Increased U.S. borrowing costs can ripple through the global economy, affecting other nations' borrowing costs and financial stability.

The rising global debt, including the significant debt burden of the United States, poses substantial risks to national and global economic stability. Addressing these challenges requires coordinated efforts to promote sustainable fiscal policies, improve debt management, and enhance economic growth. For the United States, managing the growing debt will be crucial to maintaining financial stability and ensuring a prosperous future. Reducing deficits, implementing structural reforms, and fostering economic growth are essential to mitigate the risks associated with high debt levels.

As global threats such as mounting debt, climate change, and other critical issues demand the best minds and a united front to tackle them, the growing political polarization in the United States has profound implications for the nation and its future. This divide, which has been intensifying since the 1970s, is evident in the increasing ideological distance between Democrats and Republicans. This heightened partisanship hampers legislative progress, leading to significant gridlock in Congress.

As a result, critical issues such as national debt, healthcare, immigration, and climate change remain unresolved or inadequately addressed due to the inability to reach bipartisan agreements. The lack of cooperation and compromise means that essential policy reforms are either stalled or diluted, preventing effective solutions. This undermines the country's ability to address urgent domestic problems and weakens its global position, where unified and decisive action is crucial.

Furthermore, the polarization contributes to a toxic political environment, eroding public trust in institutions and leaders. This divisiveness can lead to increased social unrest and weaken the nation's social fabric, making it more challenging to foster the collective action necessary to address these pressing global challenges. The need for bipartisan collaboration and innovative solutions has never been greater. Yet, the growing political divide threatens to paralyze efforts to create a sustainable and prosperous future for all Americans.

It has become increasingly challenging for moderate candidates from either the right or left to secure an election, as those with more extreme views often garner substantial funding and voter support. This shift is driven by the polarization of political parties and the backing of special interest groups that prefer candidates with radical views. When these extreme politicians take office, they bring their ideologies into government, affecting legislative priorities and contributing to a divided political environment.

Recent elections have highlighted this trend. For example, studies have shown that candidates with more extreme ideologies are now more likely to run for and win state offices, furthering polarization at both state and federal levels. This polarization is evident in states like Virginia and Kentucky. In Virginia, despite significant efforts from the Republican Governor, Democrats managed to retain control of the Senate and flip the House, indicating a polarized electorate responding strongly to contentious issues such as abortion rights.

Furthermore, the 2023 gubernatorial elections showcased significant wins for candidates with strong ideological positions. In Kentucky, Democratic Governor Andy Beshear won re-election in a predominantly Republican state, while in Louisiana, Republican Jeff Landry won the governorship outright, reflecting the polarized nature of modern elections.

This trend underscores how extreme candidates increasingly dominate the political landscape, sidelining moderates and leading to governance that reflects more radical positions. This growing polarization complicates bipartisan cooperation and effective policymaking, highlighting the need for reforms to reduce the influence of extreme ideologies in American politics.

Socially, polarization fosters an "us vs. them" mentality, where political opponents are considered rivals and enemies. This mentality deepens societal divisions and fuels social tensions, making political discourse increasingly stressful and unproductive. The public's frustration with politics is evident, as many Americans find political conversations more stressful than engaging, further entrenching the divide.

Living in Washington, D.C., we can acutely feel the effects of political polarization. This division is so pervasive that it extends into everyday life, influencing where people choose to live, the schools their children attend, and even the restaurants they frequent. This polarization is not just a matter of differing opinions but has become a deep social divide, with Republicans and Democrats often inhabiting separate social spheres.

A recent Pew Research Center study highlights that Americans increasingly view members of the opposing political party not just as opponents but in negative personal terms, describing them as closed-minded, dishonest, and unintelligent. This hatred makes political discourse more stressful and frustrating, with 61% of U.S. adults finding conversations with those they disagree with more aggravating than enlightening.

Moreover, this political divide is evident in residents' social habits. People tend to align with communities and institutions that reflect their political affiliations, creating environments where social and political homogeneity are the norms. This trend is bolstered by cognitive biases such as confirmation bias, where individuals seek information that reinforces their beliefs, further entrenching these divides.

The impact of polarization in D.C. mirrors broader national trends where political identity increasingly defines social identity, influencing everything from personal relationships to community engagement. The challenge of bridging this divide remains critical for fostering a more cohesive society and effective governance.

Internationally, this polarization undermines the United States' ability to maintain a cohesive foreign policy. A politically fragmented nation struggles to project a unified stance on global issues, weakening its influence and credibility on the world stage.

This internal division can embolden adversaries and reduce the trust and cooperation of international allies.

Combining the challenges of political polarization with the escalating debt issues underscores the need for comprehensive strategies that address governance and economic sustainability. Without effective management of these intertwined issues, the risks to social cohesion, financial stability, and international standing will continue to grow. If the current trend of polarization continues, the United States may face more severe domestic and global challenges. Bridging these divides and fostering cooperation is essential for ensuring the nation's stability and prosperity in the future. Political leaders and citizens alike must work toward dialogue and collaboration to navigate these complex challenges effectively.

Despite its internal challenges, the United States faces significant opportunities for positive change. While concerning, political polarization, economic inequality, and social divisions also present unique chances for growth and transformation. The immense military expenditures and extensive foreign engagements provide a backdrop against which the country can reevaluate and recalibrate its priorities.

The challenges of adapting to rapid technological changes offer the United States a platform to innovate and lead in the global tech landscape, fostering economic growth and job creation.

Addressing climate change not only tests the resilience of the American system but also presents an opportunity for the nation to pioneer sustainable practices and renewable energy solutions, positioning itself as a global leader in environmental stewardship.

By embracing these challenges with a forward-thinking approach, the United States can harness its strengths to build a more inclusive, equitable, and sustainable society. The nation's capacity for innovation, diverse population, and democratic foundations provide a solid basis for overcoming obstacles and driving positive change. Through collective effort and a commitment to addressing systemic issues, the United States has the potential to emerge stronger and more resilient, setting an example for the rest of the world.

Historical books are not just narratives of the past; they are essential tools that equip us with knowledge to navigate and shape the future more effectively.

From Facts to Fiction: The Science Behind Sci-Fi

"Any sufficiently advanced technology is indistinguishable from magic." - Arthur C. Clarke

Unlike historical knowledge, which is often extensive and detailed, the nature of scientific knowledge is inherently progressive and provisional, continuously evolving based on new discoveries. This dynamism is a fundamental characteristic of the scientific method, the cornerstone of scientific knowledge-building. Through this method, hypotheses are formulated based on existing data and are rigorously tested through experimentation and observation. These hypotheses can be either validated or refuted, leading to a perpetual cycle of refinement and enhancement of our understanding. This process underscores science's ever-evolving, self-correcting nature, distinguishing it from fields that rely more heavily on static bodies of recorded information.

Science has profoundly impacted human life, transforming societies and improving the quality of life across the globe. Science's influence is ubiquitous and multifaceted, from healthcare advancements to technological innovations.

In healthcare, scientific research has led to the development of vaccines, antibiotics, and various medical treatments that have eradicated or controlled once-fatal diseases. Vaccines have eliminated smallpox and reduced the incidence of polio, measles, and other infectious diseases. Antibiotics have revolutionized the treatment of bacterial infections, saving countless lives. Modern medical imaging technologies, such as MRI and CT scans, enable early diagnosis and treatment of illnesses, improving patient outcomes.

Technological innovations driven by science have revolutionized communication, transportation, and daily living. The invention of the internet has connected people worldwide, facilitating instant communication, access to information, and global commerce. Advances in transportation, including automobiles, airplanes, and high-speed trains, have made travel faster, safer, and more efficient, shrinking the world and fostering cultural exchange and economic growth.

In agriculture, scientific advancements have led to the development of high-yield, disease-resistant crop varieties, and sustainable farming practices. These innovations have increased food production, ensuring food security for growing populations and reducing hunger and malnutrition. Genetic engineering and biotechnology have further enhanced crop resilience and nutritional value, contributing to healthier and more sustainable food systems.

Environmental science has raised awareness of human activity's impacts on the planet and driven efforts to mitigate climate change, pollution, and biodiversity loss. Renewable energy technologies, such as solar and wind power, have emerged as viable alternatives to fossil fuels, reducing greenhouse gas emissions and promoting a sustainable energy future. Conservation efforts informed by ecological research have helped protect endangered species and preserve natural habitats.

Space exploration, a pinnacle of scientific achievement, has expanded our understanding of the universe and inspired generations. Discoveries made by space missions have provided insights into the solar system's origins, the potential for life on other planets, and the fundamental laws of physics. Technologies developed for space exploration have also found applications on Earth, from satellite communications to materials science.

Science has had an overwhelmingly positive impact on human life by addressing challenges and improving living standards. Through relentless inquiry and innovation, science continues to shape a better future for humanity. This transformative power is evident in numerous aspects of our lives.

Historically, the evolution of scientific knowledge underscores its provisional nature. Scientific consensus, while robust, has often been overturned by new evidence, reflecting the dynamic and self-correcting essence of science.

In the early 20th century, the Newtonian framework of physics was unchallenged until experiments on the photoelectric effect could not be explained by classical theories. This anomaly led to the development of quantum mechanics, fundamentally altering our understanding of atomic and subatomic processes. Similarly, the once-prevailing belief in a static universe was completely revised with Edwin Hubble's observations of the expanding universe, which provided foundational support for the Big Bang theory.

Additionally, other scientific misconceptions have been corrected over time. Lead, for example, was once widely used in products ranging from paint to plumbing due to its durability and malleability. However, it was later discovered that lead is highly toxic, leading to severe public health policies to eliminate its use in household products and gasoline. Asbestos, similarly, was once hailed for its heat resistance and used extensively in construction. Over time, its fibers were found to cause lung diseases, including cancer, prompting a major reevaluation of its use and stringent regulations on its handling.

Scientific understanding and regulatory oversight of chemicals hazardous to human health continually evolve as new research emerges. In recent years, several chemicals once considered safe have been reevaluated and identified as potentially dangerous.

One prominent example is Per- and Polyfluoroalkyl Substances (PFAS), known as "forever chemicals," which persist in the environment and human body. Initially developed for their heat, oil, and water resistance, PFAS are commonly found in products like non-stick cookware and waterproof clothing. Over time, studies have linked PFAS exposure to serious health issues, including cancer, thyroid disease, and immune system dysfunction. Despite their widespread use, the long-term environmental and health impacts were not fully understood until relatively recently.

Similarly, Bisphenol A (BPA), used in plastics and resins, was once prevalent in many consumer goods such as water bottles and food containers. It has since been identified as an endocrine disruptor with potential links to reproductive disorders, heart disease, and diabetes. This shift in understanding has led to increased regulations and the development of BPA-free products.

In parallel with these health concerns, many countries have taken significant steps to reduce plastic pollution by banning single-use plastic items. As of July 2021, the European Union has prohibited the sale of single-use plastic plates, cutlery, straws, and other items. This legislation aims to combat marine pollution and promote sustainable alternatives. Additionally, countries like England have implemented similar bans, recognizing the environmental impact of disposable plastics and the need for more responsible consumer behavior.

These measures reflect a growing global effort to address plastic pollution and its detrimental effects on human health and the environment. Countries are working towards a more sustainable and healthier future by reducing reliance on single-use plastics and promoting safer alternatives.

Glyphosate, a widely used herbicide, was considered safe for decades. However, the International Agency for Research on Cancer (IARC) now classifies it as "probably carcinogenic to humans," linking it to non-Hodgkin's lymphoma and other cancers. This reclassification has sparked global debate and legal battles over its use and labeling.

Other chemicals like Triclosan and Phthalates have also come under scrutiny. Triclosan, found in antibacterial soaps and cosmetics, is associated with hormonal disruptions and bacterial resistance. Phthalates, used to make plastics more flexible, are implicated in reproductive and developmental issues due to their properties as endocrine disruptors.

Changes in understanding are also common in medicine. For decades, ulcers were thought to be caused by stress or spicy foods. However, research in the 1980s by Barry Marshall and Robin Warren demonstrated that the bacterium Helicobacter pylori was a primary cause of most peptic ulcers, revolutionizing treatment approaches.

These examples underscore how scientific understanding can shift as new data becomes available. This ongoing process reflects the dynamic nature of the scientific inquiry, where initial hypotheses and safety assessments are continually updated, considering new evidence. It underscores the importance of robust, ongoing research and adaptive regulatory frameworks based on the best available science to protect public health. Continuous revision and refinement are crucial to advancing our knowledge and correcting past misconceptions, highlighting the ever-evolving pursuit of scientific truth.

The digital age has accelerated the rate of scientific discovery, allowing for rapid data collection and analysis, which leads to faster revisions of existing theories. For example, genetics has seen significant advances in the past decade, with technologies like CRISPR offering new insights into gene editing that were not conceivable before.

Despite these advancements, the pursuit of scientific knowledge remains an ongoing process. Each discovery adds to the body of knowledge but also raises new questions. The recent detection of gravitational waves, predicted by Einstein a century ago, not only confirmed aspects of his theories but also opened new avenues of research into the cosmos.

In essence, science's trajectory is one of continual learning and adaptation. No claim to absolute knowledge is possible; science thrives on a dynamic of testing, falsifying, and refining ideas. This method has proven the best way to approach the truth, even as it acknowledges the provisional nature of current understanding. This humility in the face of the vast unknown drives the scientific endeavor forward, ever-expanding the frontiers of human knowledge.

On the other hand, science fiction has long served as a fertile ground for the seeds of future technological advancements, acting as a critical incubator for ideas that stretch and challenge our notions of what is technologically and socially feasible. This genre transcends mere entertainment; it offers imaginative explorations that often become the blueprint for real-world innovation. Through its narratives, science fiction has the unique ability to envision future technologies and societal changes, from space travel and robotics to virtual reality and artificial intelligence. These speculative visions often inspire scientists, engineers, and entrepreneurs to turn what once seemed impossible into reality, propelling technological and social progress. By imagining the future, science fiction not only shapes our expectations but also influences the development of new technologies and frameworks for how we might interact with them and each other.

One of the most iconic examples of science fiction's influence on technology is the communicator from "Star Trek," which premiered in the 1960s. These devices, functionally similar to today's mobile phones, appeared when telephones were anything but portable. Martin Cooper, the engineer who led the team that developed Motorola's first handheld mobile phone, has cited "Star Trek's" communicators as a direct inspiration. This instance demonstrates how science fiction can ignite the imaginations of technologists and scientists, guiding them to turn fanciful concepts into tangible technologies.

Another profound influence can be seen in the gestural interfaces featured in Steven Spielberg's film "Minority Report." During production, the film's team consulted extensively with scientists and technologists to base its speculative technology on feasible science. The interfaces designed for the film have inspired real-world technologies in touch and gesture-based systems, fundamentally impacting how we interact with devices today, from smartphones to gaming consoles.

Ridley Scott's "Blade Runner" offers yet another vision, depicting a world inhabited by bioengineered beings and sophisticated artificial intelligence. This narrative exploration has become increasingly relevant as AI and synthetic biology advancements evolve. "Blade Runner" probes into the ethical dilemmas and societal impacts of such technologies—themes that we are grappling with more tangibly today.

The influence of science fiction also extends into the realm of ethical considerations. Series like "Black Mirror" provide cautionary tales about the potential pitfalls of our reliance on technology, exploring how future innovations might affect privacy, autonomy, and social dynamics. These narratives are vital for shaping public discourse around the ethical implications of emerging technologies, urging us to consider the broader consequences of our technological endeavors.

This reciprocal relationship between science fiction and real-world technology constitutes a dynamic, ongoing dialogue—a visionary cycle that enhances imaginative storytelling and technological innovation. This symbiosis fosters the creation of new technologies and encourages thoughtful consideration of how these technologies integrate into society.

Recently, science fiction films have increasingly explored elaborate visions of the future, delving into complex themes such as space travel, life integrated with advanced AI technologies, and other futuristic concepts. These films are not only a testament to the creative ability of their directors but also reflect a profound understanding of scientific possibilities, making them more realistic and meaningful portrayals of future realities.

Space travel, a classic staple of science fiction, has been

reimagined with greater technical detail and plausibility. Films like "Interstellar" and "The Martian" showcase this evolution. "Interstellar," directed by Christopher Nolan, explores concepts of wormholes, black holes, and time dilation with input from theoretical physicist Kip Thorne, ensuring the scientific underpinnings are as accurate as possible within the narrative context. "The Martian," directed by Ridley Scott and based on Andy Weir's novel, presents a meticulously detailed survival story on Mars, grounded in current space travel technology and botany.

Artificial intelligence is another area where recent science fiction movies have excelled in blending complex ideas with engaging storytelling. Movies like "Ex Machina" and "Her" investigate AI's ethical and emotional dimensions, pushing the audience to ponder the nature of consciousness and personal relationships in the age of artificial intelligence. "Ex Machina" delves into the implications of creating a machine with human-like awareness, focusing on the moral and psychological consequences. At the same time, "Her" explores the emotional depth of a relationship between a human and an operating system, highlighting issues of intimacy and connection in a digital age.

Moreover, these films often discuss the societal impacts of future technologies. "Blade Runner 2049" extends the themes of its predecessor by examining the moral implications of bioengineered humans and the environmental and socio-economic contexts that such technologies could engender. This sequel deepens the discussion about identity, memory, and humanity in a world where the lines between human and machine are increasingly blurred.

"Atlas," a Netflix original film, is another sci-fi movie set twenty-eight years after a transformative AI experiment in a future dominated by advanced AI. The plot follows Atlas, a counterterrorism analyst and the daughter of the scientist who sparked this AI revolution. She confronts a rogue AI, her "brother," who has instigated a robot uprising and become an AI terrorist.

Taking place on the hostile planet GR39, the movie showcases advanced technology, such as Atlas's mechanical battle armor, which is crucial for her survival and features integrated combat, surveillance, and communication systems. The film also highlights futuristic hologram visualizations, which are used extensively for both strategic operations and daily interactions, adding a layer of depth to the digital immersion of the storyline.

The screenplay by acclaimed sci-fi author Alex Mercer explores the ethical dilemmas of AI autonomy and the unforeseen consequences of artificial intelligence surpassing human control. Mercer's narrative probes the complex interplay between technology and morality, presenting a poignant examination of the balance between human governance and autonomous machines.

"Atlas" merges thought-provoking themes with high-tech

futurism, including the mesmerizing use of holograms as visual displays. It invites viewers to reflect on the complex relationship between humans and their AI creations, portraying a future deeply entangled with artificial intelligence.

The directors of these films collaborate closely with scientists, engineers, and futurists to build worlds that are not only visually stunning but also scientifically plausible. This collaboration helps create a more immersive and intellectually stimulating experience, drawing audiences into a future that could realistically emerge. This level of detail and sophistication in storytelling entertains, educates, and provokes thoughtful discussion among viewers about our technological trajectory and its potential consequences for society.

The recent trend in science fiction cinema towards creating elaborate and realistic visions of the future serves a dual purpose: it offers a spectacular glimpse into potential tomorrows while prompting critical reflection on the technological and ethical dilemmas we face today. This makes modern science fiction films not merely a mirror reflecting our collective hopes and fears about the future but also a lens through which visionary filmmakers help us evaluate our society's possible paths. These narratives challenge us to think deeply about our choices and responsibilities in shaping the future, highlighting the power of cinema to entertain and inspire, and provoke thoughtful discussion.

My profound appreciation for science fiction has always been rooted in its dual role as both a predictor of the future and an inspirer of reality. The genre uniquely merges creativity with scientific insight, acting as a catalyst for change and continuously pushing the boundaries of what is possible, urging us toward the next significant breakthrough. This intricate interplay of imagination and reality underscores science fiction's enduring impact, highlighting its critical role in shaping the future.

SHAHIN SAMADI

Shaping Tomorrow: The Transformative Power of Technological Innovation

"Innovation distinguishes between a leader and a follower." - Steve Jobs

Revolutionary change has shaped human history, and each epoch is defined by profound technological, cultural, and social structure shifts. From the dawn of civilization in the Stone Age to the transformative Industrial Revolution, these pivotal moments have reshaped societies and laid the foundation for the modern world. While many of these revolutions unfolded over centuries, the pace of change has accelerated dramatically recently, driven by rapid technological advancements.

As we stand on the precipice of a new era characterized by the relentless march of innovation, it becomes increasingly evident that we are entering a period of more frequent and profound revolutionary cycles. The staggering pace of technological progress and the dynamic nature of modern society demand that humans remain adaptable and agile in the face of change.

Indeed, the significant differences between generations are a moving reminder of the imperative to embrace adaptation and evolution. As each new wave of innovation reshapes the landscape of human experience, those who fail to adapt risk being left behind. Thus, the ability to anticipate and adeptly respond to technological advancements becomes paramount in navigating the complexities of the modern world.

In this ever-evolving landscape, the key to staying ahead lies in a willingness to embrace change and harness the transformative power of innovation. By remaining vigilant, proactive, and open-minded, humans can survive and thrive amidst the swirling currents of revolution that define our age.

The Stone Age, encompassing both the Paleolithic and Neolithic periods, marked the dawn of human innovation with the development of the first stone tools. These tools represented a profound shift in human capability and behavior. During the Paleolithic era, our ancestors were primarily hunter-gatherers, reliant on what the environment offered for sustenance. The introduction of stone tools enhanced their efficiency in hunting, gathering, and, later, food processing. This evolutionary path led to the Neolithic Revolution, around 10,000 BCE, which humanity's first major agricultural breakthrough. The transition from nomadic lifestyles to settled farming enabled the growth of stable communities, setting the stage for developing villages and, eventually, complex societies.

Following the Stone Age, the Bronze Age Revolution began

around 3300 BCE with the discovery of metallurgy, particularly the creation of bronze—a mixture of copper and tin. This advancement allowed for the production of stronger tools and weapons than those made purely from stone, catalyzing changes in agriculture, warfare, and art. Societies became more stratified and organized, giving rise to distinct classes and professions. The ability to manipulate metals also led to the development of expansive trade networks and the expansion of cultural and technological exchanges, enhancing communication and interaction between distant civilizations.

The progression continued into the Iron Age around 1200 BCE when iron began to replace bronze in producing tools and weapons. Iron ore, more abundant than the tin and copper required for bronze, became a pivotal resource, fostering significant advancements in agricultural productivity, military might, and architectural possibilities. These developments supported more complex states characterized by sophisticated administrative structures.

The increasing complexity of societies led to the rise of the first urban centers in regions like Mesopotamia, Egypt, and along the Indus River around 3500 BCE. This urban revolution saw the creation of cities, which became centers of trade, religion, and government, further stimulating cultural and technological advancements. These urban centers were heavily reliant on agricultural surplus, which fueled local and long-distance trade, reinforcing the interconnectedness of ancient civilizations.

These historical advancements culminated in the Industrial Revolution, which began in the late 18th century in Britain—this period marked a dramatic turning point in human history, with wide-reaching effects on social, economic, and cultural conditions worldwide. Powered by the invention of steam engines, the development of factories, and the mechanization of agriculture, the Industrial Revolution triggered a shift from agricultural economies to industrial powerhouses. The mass production of goods led to improved living standards but also introduced new challenges, such as urbanization, environmental degradation, and the rise of a factory-based working class.

These revolutions, from the crafting of stone tools to the steam-powered industrial age, illustrate the remarkable journey of human societies. Each stage is built upon past innovations, showcasing our unending quest to reshape and improve our conditions through the ages.

The Second Industrial Revolution, often called the Technological Revolution, was a phase of rapid industrialization in the final third of the 19th century and the beginning of the 20th century. This period marked a significant evolution beyond the initial Industrial Revolution that began in Britain in the late 18th century.

The Second Industrial Revolution, marked by significant advancements in manufacturing and production technology, catalyzed profound changes in steel, electric power, and petroleum industries. This era brought about transformative developments that reshaped industry, transportation, and daily life.

A significant hallmark of this period was the mass production of steel, facilitated by innovations like the Bessemer process and the open-hearth furnace. Steel, more durable and stronger than iron, became fundamental in building modern infrastructure, including railroads, bridges, buildings, and manufacturing machinery and ships. This robust material supported an infrastructure boom that symbolized modern progress.

Electrification also played a critical role during this time. The introduction and spread of electric power fundamentally changed how factories operated, making them more efficient than those powered by steam or water from the First Industrial Revolution. Thomas Edison's invention of the electric light bulb in 1879, followed by the development of electrical grids, extended the working day and significantly enhanced the quality of life in homes and workplaces, marking the beginning of a new era in energy usage.

This period saw groundbreaking innovations in chemistry, including the development of synthetic dyes and the creation of fertilizers. These chemical processes boosted agricultural productivity and supported rapid population growth, providing the necessary resources for an expanding society.

The refinement of the internal combustion engine was another pivotal development, leading to the rise of automobiles and airplanes in the early 20th century. Initially running on gas and later on petroleum-based fuels such as gasoline, the engine revolutionized transportation, enabling faster travel times and greater personal and commercial mobility.

Telecommunications also saw significant advancements, notably with Alexander Graham Bell's invention of the telephone in 1876. This breakthrough dramatically changed long-distance communication, making it almost instantaneous and reshaping social and business interactions.

These innovations during the Second Industrial Revolution transformed societies and economies worldwide, paving the way for modern industrial landscapes and setting the stage for the technological advances of the 20th century.

The Second Industrial Revolution increased productivity and an economic boom in many parts of the world, particularly in the United States and Germany, which began challenging British industrial supremacy. The era saw the rise of large industrial corporations and complex organizational structures. Urbanization accelerated as people moved from rural areas to cities to work in factories, and this shift had profound social implications, including the growth of a distinct working class and changes in living conditions.

The proliferation of industries and the growth of the factory system also heightened the need for regulatory reforms, as seen in the labor movements advocating for better working conditions, shorter hours, and better wages; this period laid the groundwork for the modern industrial economy and the complex social dynamics defining the 20th century.

Each evolution has contributed to human civilization's intricate and layered fabric, setting the stage for subsequent technological and social developments. From Stone Age toolmaking to the sophisticated industrial machinery of the modern era, these revolutionary periods reflect a relentless pursuit of improvement and adaptation that continues to drive human progress today.

While some evolutions, such as the transition from the Stone Age to the Bronze Age, took thousands of years, we now witness technological advancements that can profoundly impact society within just a few decades or even a single generation. This accelerated pace of innovation, exemplified by developments in digital technology, biotechnology, and artificial intelligence, promises to reshape our future more rapidly than ever.

CURRENTS OF BEING

Growing up during the Digital Revolution, also known as the Third Industrial Revolution, I witnessed a pivotal era that began in the latter half of the 20th century and continues to reshape our lives. This revolution is defined by a seismic shift from mechanical and analog electronic technology to digital electronics, a transition that began with the proliferation of digital computers and digital record-keeping after the Second World War.

The roots of this digital transformation trace back to the 1950s with the invention of the transistor, a development that dramatically advanced the capability of electronic devices by making them smaller, cheaper, and more efficient. The creation of the microprocessor in the 1970s further accelerated this trend, laying the foundational technology for the personal computer. By the late 1970s and early 1980s, personal computing began to take hold in everyday life, with iconic machines like the Apple II and the IBM PC making technology accessible to the masses, thereby democratizing computer usage across businesses and households alike.

Another monumental advancement was the rise of the Internet. Initially developed as a military and academic network in the 1960s, the Internet burst into the public sphere in the 1990s, rapidly evolving into an essential global infrastructure for communication and commerce. Tim Berners-Lee's introduction of the World Wide Web in 1989 revolutionized its functionality, transforming it into a dynamic multimedia platform that integrates text, graphics, and sound, making information and connectivity accessible like never before.

The late 1990s and early 2000s marked the advent of mobile computing, with the emergence of smartphones that melded the computer's functionality with the connectivity of a telephone. Concurrently, the development of cloud computing meant that data and services could be hosted not on personal machines but in remote data centers accessible via the Internet. This shift has enabled the rapid growth of big data, artificial intelligence, and machine learning, reshaping business models, elevating security concerns, and redefining data governance.

The social and economic impacts of the Digital Revolution are profound, transforming industries from manufacturing to services like finance, education, and healthcare. It has fundamentally altered how businesses operate and deliver products and services. Moreover, it has reshaped social interactions, media consumption, and political engagement through platforms like Facebook, YouTube, and Twitter, illustrating the sweeping influence of digital technology in modern life.

The Digital Revolution has brought about profound changes that continue to influence every aspect of human life. As this revolution evolves, it promises even greater shifts in how we connect, understand the world, and manage emerging challenges in the information age.

During my college years, I spent countless hours in the library conducting academic research for my undergraduate and graduate courses and my PhD dissertation. This process often involved navigating through index cards to locate the appropriate books. If I were fortunate enough to find the right book, I would search for specific pages containing the information I needed. The required materials were sometimes unavailable in my university's library, necessitating trips to other academic institutions and sometimes even the Library of Congress.

As technology progressed, the situation began to improve. Many libraries started offering online access to a wide array of research papers and academic materials, which significantly enhanced the accessibility and efficiency of academic research.

Today, the landscape of academic research has transformed even further. Modern researchers have advanced applications and powerful search engines that allow them to access the materials they need with just a few clicks. This technological evolution has not only streamlined the research process but has also made a wealth of information readily accessible, thereby enhancing the efficiency and depth of academic inquiries.

When I took my first computer course in the early 1980s, the technology was relatively primitive by today's standards. We used to type our programs onto punch cards, requiring meticulous attention to detail. Each card held a line of code, and we would carry boxes filled with these cards to be fed into card readers. These readers would then input the codes into an IBM mainframe housed in a large, specially designed computer room. Remarkably, that entire mainframe had less computing power than today's Apple Watch. This stark comparison highlights just how rapidly technology has advanced over the decades.

When I took over the management of the GWU computer center, I was part of a pioneering group that had the unique opportunity to collaborate with Apple during the nascent stages of their computer production. Apple generously provided us with a dozen of their first-edition computers. This experience marked a significant milestone in the university's technological advancements and placed us at the forefront of educational institutions integrating cutting-edge technology into their curriculum. This collaboration with Apple clearly indicated the transformative changes starting to take shape in the computing world during that era.

Additionally, we expanded our technology infrastructure by acquiring Hewlett-Packard (HP) and Digital Equipment Systems (DEC) for the engineering school. These systems, known as minicomputers, were well-suited to the specific needs of the scientific and engineering curriculum. They provided the necessary computing power and versatility required for various engineering applications. With these additions, our engineering school's computer room soon boasted a diverse array of computing resources, ensuring students had access to various technologies to complete their assignments effectively. This investment significantly enhanced the educational tools at our disposal, allowing students to explore and learn with state-of-the-art equipment at their fingertips.

When I began my tenure at NASA, our facility was equipped primarily with several robust DEC minicomputer systems, which also had access to other NASA supercomputer resources. During this period, our center was at the forefront of the emerging Internet era, serving as one of the initial nodes in a nationwide networked system that, at the time, was limited primarily to government agencies and educational institutions. This early version of the Internet was a crucial tool for collaboration and data sharing among researchers and scientists, paving the way for the expansive global network we rely on today. Our involvement in these pioneering efforts marked a significant chapter in the history of computing and communications technology.

Shortly after my career started at NASA, representatives from Silicon Graphics and Sun Microsystems approached us with an offer to provide several of their powerful Unix-based workstations. These systems were renowned for their robust performance in graphical processing and complex computational tasks, which were ideal for our advanced research and development projects.

Silicon Graphics, often known for its high-performance computing and graphical systems, later partnered with Cray. Together, they developed advanced visualization capabilities for Cray's supercomputers, leveraging Silicon Graphics' expertise in graphics and multimedia. This collaboration contributed to some of the most powerful supercomputing resources available, enhancing our capabilities for handling large-scale scientific computations and visualizations. This period marked a significant evolution in computing power and capability, directly impacting the scope and scale of research initiatives at our center.

At NASA, we were privileged to have access to some of the most advanced computing systems in the world, specifically tailored for our scientific research. This technological advantage kept us at the forefront of innovation, consistently ahead of the curve in various fields of study. These powerful computers enabled us to conduct complex simulations, process extensive data sets, and execute intricate calculations quickly and accurately. This access accelerated our research capabilities and allowed us to pioneer new technologies and methodologies, solidifying NASA's position as a scientific and technological advancement leader.

In turn, I had the privilege of being an integral part of the technological revolution, teaching and applying some of the most advanced technological innovations in the world. My role allowed me to witness the rapid evolution of technology firsthand and contribute to groundbreaking projects that pushed the boundaries of what was scientifically and practically achievable. This experience deepened my understanding of complex systems and enabled me to share cutting-edge knowledge and practices with others, fostering a culture of innovation and learning. Being at the forefront of these developments was both a responsibility and an honor, as each advancement could significantly impact our understanding of the world and improve our way of life.

Since 2000, there has been a noticeable shift in the locus of technological innovation from government agencies to the private sector. This transition was marked by an increasing number of technology companies driving innovation directly into the consumer market, a change from the previous era where much of the pioneering research and development in technology was spearheaded by government or government-funded entities.

Historically, many foundational technologies such as the internet, GPS, and even touchscreen technology were developed under government projects and funding. Agencies such as NASA, the Department of Defense, and DARPA (Defense Advanced Research Projects Agency) were instrumental in the early stages of core technologies in today's consumer electronics and services.

However, from the start of the 21st century, Silicon Valley's dynamism—fueled by venture capital investment and an entrepreneurial culture—began to take a more prominent role in technological innovation. Companies like Apple, Google, and Facebook (now Meta), and later Tesla and Uber, have driven much of their research and development, focusing on consumer needs and commercial markets. This includes advancements in artificial intelligence, machine learning, mobile computing, and renewable energy technologies.

The innovation landscape has undergone significant changes, primarily due to the dynamic roles that private companies play in driving technological advancements globally. Unlike government entities, which are often slowed by bureaucratic processes, private companies are motivated by competition and profit, enabling them to bring products and innovations to market quickly. This agility has accelerated the pace of technological adoption worldwide, making new technologies available more rapidly than ever before.

Private firms' research and development (R&D) investment has substantially increased, surpassing traditional government spending. This surge in investment has fueled a wave of innovation and attracted a global pool of talent to tech hubs like Seattle and

Silicon Valley. These regions have become melting pots of creativity and technological breakthroughs, drawing the best minds from around the world.

Private companies typically focus on developing technologies that offer immediate commercial viability and address specific consumer needs. This consumer-centric approach contrasts with government projects, which often target broader scientific goals or longer-term research that may have little market applications. As a result, technologies developed by private enterprises tend to reach consumers faster and are more tailored to their immediate needs.

The economic impact of these private sector innovations has been profound, particularly in regions like Silicon Valley. The technological boom has not only created numerous jobs but has also contributed significantly to GDP growth. These regions have become powerhouses of economic activity, driven by continuous innovations in the tech sector.

Furthermore, companies based in tech hubs have begun to influence global technology trends and policies significantly. Their reach affects various aspects of global governance, from privacy laws to international trade agreements, reflecting their growing power internationally.

However, this shift from government-led to private sector-driven innovation is not without its challenges. Privacy concerns, data security, and the monopolistic tendencies of large tech firms have emerged as significant concerns. These companies often dominate multiple aspects of consumer lives, raising questions about their influence and the potential sidelining of less commercially viable technologies that could be crucial for societal advancement.

While the transition of innovation from government to the private sector has democratized technology access and created unprecedented economic and social opportunities, it has also changed how we live and work. This shift necessitates careful regulation and foresight to ensure that the benefits of such innovations are balanced against the need to protect the public interest and promote societal good.

Our company, INNOVIM, leverages the latest and innovative technologies, including artificial intelligence, machine learning, and cloud computing, to address some of the most challenging aspects of our clients, mostly government agencies' mission-critical problems. Our approach involves harnessing these advanced tools to analyze vast amounts of data, optimize processes, and deliver solutions that are not only efficient but also transformative. By integrating these cutting-edge technologies into our workflows, we empower our clients to achieve significant breakthroughs in their operations, enhancing both their effectiveness and competitive edge in their respective fields. This commitment to innovation and excellence positions INNOVIM as a leader in solving complex, high-stakes challenges with precision and ingenuity.

As a key member of the technology revolution, I have witnessed the exponential growth of technology and its remarkable benefits to humanity. The advancements in fields such as artificial intelligence, cloud computing, and machine learning have allowed us to tackle many previously impossible problems. This rapid evolution has expanded our capabilities and transformed how we approach and solve critical issues across various sectors. By leveraging cutting-edge technologies, we can find solutions more efficiently and with greater precision, addressing challenges that were once only dreamt of solving. This era of technological innovation continues to push the boundaries of possibility, significantly enhancing our quality of life and understanding of the world.

We are still in the early stages of understanding how technology will fundamentally transform our lives. The advent of self-improving or self-adaptive AI represents a significant leap forward in making technologies more intuitive and efficient. These AI systems can analyze their performance, learn from interactions, and autonomously enhance their algorithms without human intervention, leading to more intelligent and responsive solutions.

Furthermore, the emergence of optical technology opens up new frontiers in processing speeds and energy efficiency. Optical technology promises to drastically reduce current hardware's heat and power limitations by using light instead of electrical signals to transmit information, enabling faster, more complex computations while consuming less energy.

In the rapidly advancing realm of technology, quantum computing stands at the forefront as a revolutionary force. Unlike classical computers, which operate on binary code systems rooted in 20th-century transistor technology, quantum computers exploit the unique principles of quantum mechanics to address problems of unprecedented complexity.

While supercomputers are potent, they can struggle with highly intricate problems characterized by numerous variables interacting in complex ways. Quantum computers, on the other hand, harness qubits, which can simultaneously embody multiple states until observed. At their core are quantum bits, or qubits, which can exist simultaneously in a superposition of one and zero until measured. Although still in their early stages, quantum computers are a tangible reality, with numerous technology companies offering access to programming languages and resources for software development.

The property, known as quantum superposition, combined

with the phenomenon of entanglement (where states of multiple qubits are quantum mechanically linked), grants quantum computers capabilities beyond the reach of classical counterparts. Both classical and quantum computers possess chips, circuits, and logic gates, and both rely on algorithms and utilize a binary code of ones and zeros to process information. However, the fundamental physical encoding of information takes a radically different form.

Quantum computers have the potential to perform certain types of calculations much faster than classical computers. This speed advantage arises from their ability to leverage quantum superposition and entanglement, which classical computers cannot do. Therefore, Quantum computing can revolutionize various sectors, including government agencies that we support.

As we continue to integrate advanced technologies like quantum computing, artificial intelligence (AI), and robotics across various sectors, from healthcare to transportation, we are beginning to see a transformation in how operations are streamlined, decision-making processes are enhanced, and new opportunities for innovation are being created. These developments promise a future where technology supports and actively enhances every aspect of our lives.

Quantum Computing will be making a significant impact across several fields. In the pharmaceutical industry, for example, it has the potential to accelerate the drug development process significantly. By simulating molecular interactions at a quantum level, quantum computing allows researchers to identify new drug candidates more quickly and cost-effectively than ever. In the financial sector, quantum algorithms could revolutionize portfolio management and risk assessment by efficiently analyzing vast datasets and simulating economic outcomes under various scenarios. Additionally, while quantum computing presents new challenges in cybersecurity—potentially breaking many of today's encryption methods—it paves the way for more secure, quantum-resistant cryptography.

Artificial Intelligence (AI) has a broad and profound impact across multiple industries, significantly changing consumers' lives. In healthcare, AI technologies personalize treatment plans, predict patient outcomes, and assist in complex surgeries through enhanced imaging and precision techniques. AI-powered diagnostic tools improve the accuracy and speed of medical diagnoses, leading to better patient outcomes. In transportation, AI optimizes traffic flow, enhances autonomous vehicles' safety features, and improves management of public transportation systems. AI also transforms the automotive industry by developing self-driving cars, promising safer and more efficient transportation. For businesses, AI-driven analytics tools are essential for extracting valuable insights from large datasets, enabling more informed decision-making, predicting consumer behavior, and automating routine tasks. In retail, AI algorithms analyze consumer behavior to offer tailored product recommendations, enhancing the shopping experience. This era of AI innovation continues to push the boundaries of possibility, significantly enhancing our quality of life and understanding of the world.

An example of AI's impact is in sports, such as the 2024 UEFA European Championship. The official match ball, Adidas AIRODOME, has AI sensors that provide real-time data on ball speed, trajectory, and player interactions. This technology enhances the viewing experience for fans, offers valuable insights for coaches and players, and ensures fair play through accurate, instantaneous decision-making by referees.

AI is transforming music creation by composing original pieces in various styles and genres. For example, AI composers like AIVA can generate classical music pieces used in video games, advertisements, and live orchestral performances. Another AI, MuseNet by OpenAI, can create complex compositions blending styles from classical to modern pop, showcasing the versatility and creativity AI can bring to music.

In visual art, AI is pushing the boundaries of creativity. The AI-generated portrait "Edmond de Belamy," created using a Generative Adversarial Network, sold for a substantial sum at auction, highlighting the market's recognition of AI art. Additionally, platforms like DeepArt and DeepDream use neural networks to transform photos into artworks in the style of famous painters or produce surreal and abstract visuals, respectively, demonstrating AI's capability to create visually stunning and unique pieces.

AI also makes waves even in the fragrance industry by designing personalized perfumes. IBM's AI system, Philyra, analyzes vast formulas and raw materials datasets to create unique fragrances tailored to individual preferences. The Brazilian company O Boticário used this technology to develop new perfumes, showing how AI can innovate and personalize the creation of fragrances. By considering user preferences and historical data, AI can identify novel combinations that a human perfumer might miss, leading to the development of truly personalized and innovative scents.

Generative and natural language processing (NLP) AI tools, like ChatGPT, are revolutionizing consumer interactions by making digital communication more intuitive and efficient. These AI-driven tools enhance customer service with 24/7 virtual assistants, democratize access to information through language translation, and accelerate content creation by assisting writers and creators. They also offer personalized experiences across shopping, learning, and healthcare while improving security with advanced authentication methods. By integrating these technologies into daily life, consumers benefit from increased convenience, efficiency, and personalized support, making sophisticated AI assistance an essential part of modern living.

AI is also making significant strides in computer science by assisting programmers in writing code. A notable example is GitHub Copilot, an AI-powered coding assistant developed by GitHub in collaboration with OpenAI. Copilot leverages machine learning models trained on vast amounts of open-source code to suggest entire lines or blocks of code as programmers type their codes. It can autocomplete functions, provide code snippets for everyday tasks, and even assist in writing tests and documentation. This tool accelerates the coding process, reduces repetitive tasks, and allows developers to focus on the more complex aspects of their projects.

Another example is OpenAI's Codex, the model behind GitHub Copilot. Codex can understand and generate code in multiple programming languages using natural language prompts. Developers can describe what they want the code to do in plain English, and Codex can generate the corresponding code. This functionality makes coding more accessible to non-programmers and helps experienced developers prototype and test ideas quickly.

These AI tools are transforming the software development process, making it more efficient and enabling developers to

155

produce higher-quality code with fewer errors. By automating routine coding tasks, AI allows programmers to concentrate on innovative and complex aspects of their work.

These examples highlight how AI reshapes industries and enriches everyday consumer experiences, underscoring its transformative potential in our lives.

Robotics is transforming sectors with its ability to increase efficiency, reduce human error, and handle tasks that are too dangerous for humans. In manufacturing, robots lead to safer work environments and higher product quality by taking on hazardous tasks. In agriculture, robotics technology automates routine tasks such as harvesting, weeding, and planting, increasing yield and reducing reliance on pesticides and manual labor. Furthermore, in disaster response, robots are increasingly used for search and rescue operations in environments that are too risky for human responders, improving both response times and outcomes in emergencies.

Together, these transformative technologies are enhancing human capabilities, improving efficiency, and solving problems that were once considered unsolvable. This heralds a new era of technological advancement that promises to reshape every sector, driving unprecedented innovation and efficiency.

Over the years, technological advancements have radically transformed how we work and live, from simple tools like typewriters and calculators to complex systems like advanced mobile phones and GPS navigation. This progression underscores a broader trend: technology complements and increasingly replaces human labor across various domains, often performing tasks more efficiently and effectively.

In medical diagnostics, for instance, advanced algorithms and machine learning systems can now analyze complex medical data, such as imaging and genetic information, with a level of precision and speed unattainable by human practitioners alone. These technologies are improving diagnostic accuracy, enabling earlier detection of diseases, and tailoring treatments to individual patients, which optimizes outcomes and reduces costs.

Weather forecasting has benefited significantly from technology, with predictive models and data analytics becoming increasingly sophisticated. Today's systems integrate vast amounts of data from satellites, sensors, and other sources to enhance the accuracy of weather predictions. This helps in everyday planning and is crucial for preparing for severe weather events, potentially saving lives and minimizing economic impacts.

At INNOVIM, we developed a pioneering AI application called LEARN2, designed to predict extreme weather more efficiently than traditional methods. Leveraging advanced machine learning techniques, LEARN2 integrates data from leading US and international Numerical Weather Prediction centers, enhancing the accuracy of rainfall forecasts up to 10 days in advance. This tool is particularly effective in predicting the behavior of atmospheric rivers, which can lead to significant precipitation events, such as the fatal Montecito landslide and the Oroville Dam spillway erosion. LEARN2 helps improve decision-making for water management and disaster preparednessby providing earlier and more accurate warnings.

Transportation is another area undergoing a technological revolution. Autonomous vehicles, whether cars, airplanes, or ships, leverage sensors, data, and advanced algorithms to navigate safely. Self-driving cars, for instance, aim to reduce human error, the leading cause of most road accidents. Autonomous piloting and navigation systems in aviation and maritime sectors enhance safety, improve efficiency, and reduce operational costs by optimizing routes and fuel usage.

While the rise of technology in these roles presents challenges, particularly in job displacement, it also opens up new opportunities for human workers to engage in more creative, supervisory, and technical roles, overseeing and complementing the work done by machines. This transition calls for a shift in skills development and education to prepare the workforce for new jobs that emerging technologies create. As we continue to harness these innovations, they promise to enhance our capabilities and usher in new levels of efficiency and safety across multiple sectors.

The continuous development of adaptive technologies is poised to significantly reshape human cognitive and functional areas. As we increasingly rely on technology to remember details and perform calculations—tasks our brains used to manage—we may see a shift in how we use our cognitive abilities. There's a growing concern that reliance on technologies for essential memory functions, like remembering phone numbers or directions, might lead to diminished memory capabilities. Additionally, as technology delivers results instantaneously, it could foster impatience and reduced attention spans, particularly in new generations accustomed to the rapid gratification of social media and instant communication.

In today's interconnected world, virtually everyone is tethered to a smartphone, laden with many applications that enhance connectivity and continuously gather and transmit a vast array of personal data. Each digital footprint is meticulously logged, from our real-time locations and the photos we capture to our conversations and interactions on social media platforms. Moreover, our electronic devices, whether home assistants, fitness trackers, or even smart appliances, are increasingly linked to the cloud, integrating our daily activities deeper into the digital fabric.

This seamless integration into the digital realm has transformed us into unwitting commodities for major corporations.

These entities harvest and analyze our data, creating detailed profiles monetized in various ways. Companies might sell this information to advertisers who seek to tailor their marketing strategies to specific demographics' preferences or use the data to develop and refine their products and services, thus perpetuating a consumption and data generation cycle.

The implications of this data commodification raise significant privacy concerns. Often, the exchange of personal information for convenient services occurs without explicit consent or a comprehensive understanding by users of how extensively their data is being used. As a result, we are not only consumers of products but also the product itself, packaged and sold in the ever-expanding digital marketplace. This dynamic prompts critical questions about privacy rights and the need for more stringent regulations to protect personal information in the digital age.

Furthermore, the same technologies designed to enhance human life can be exploited maliciously. As our dependency on digital platforms grows, so does our vulnerability to cyber threats. Cybersecurity attacks are becoming more sophisticated as criminals and malicious agents harness advanced technology to orchestrate their activities. These include financial fraud and data theft as well as more complex cyber espionage and infrastructure attacks.

The dual use of technology means that as it evolves to assist us, it simultaneously provides increasingly robust tools for criminals to manage and expand their activities. The landscape of cyber threats is expected to grow, requiring more advanced cybersecurity measures. Governments, businesses, and individuals must invest in more robust cybersecurity defenses and foster a deeper understanding of digital safety practices. This includes developing more sophisticated security protocols and training users in cybersecurity awareness to counteract these threats effectively.

As technology develops, it is crucial to balance its benefits with potential risks, ensuring its advancements continue to serve humanity positively while mitigating adverse effects on our cognitive skills and security.

As we move beyond this Digital Revolution, the horizon is marked by several other emerging technological trends and theories that suggest profound transformations in human societies, economies, and biological makeup. These potential changes are often framed within the context of the Fourth Industrial Revolution and subsequent phases, characterized by the deep integration of digital, biological, and physical technologies.

Integration of AI and Machine Learning: The continued development and integration of artificial intelligence and machine learning into various facets of life and industry signal a future where decision-making processes are increasingly automated. This trend could enhance efficiency across multiple domains, including more intelligent urban planning, autonomous transportation systems, personalized medicine, and advanced manufacturing processes, leading to more responsive and optimized systems.

The Internet of Things (IoT) and Smart Cities: The expansion of IoT, which involves connecting everyday objects to the Internet to send and receive data, is poised to transform daily living and working environments. In smart cities, such connectivity could optimize traffic flow, energy usage, and public safety through real-time, AI-driven systems, thereby redefining urban living.

Biotechnology and Genetic Engineering: Advances in these fields pave the way toward eradicating genetic diseases, extending human lifespans, and significantly enhancing human capabilities. Techniques like CRISPR, which simplifies gene editing, make these changes more feasible and open up unprecedented possibilities for human evolution.

Neurotechnology and Human Enhancement: Innovations in neurotechnology, including brain-computer interfaces, could revolutionize human cognition and sensory experiences. These technologies can enhance memory, augment cognitive abilities, or even download skills directly to the brain, mirroring concepts often found in science fiction.

Quantum Computing: Although still in its early stages,

quantum computing is expected to bring revolutionary changes across various fields by processing information in fundamentally novel ways. This could lead to significant advancements in materials science, complex system modeling, secure communications, and problem-solving capabilities far exceeding those of current digital computers.

Decentralized Systems and Blockchain: The proliferation of blockchain technology points to a shift towards more decentralized and transparent systems. This technology could radically transform sectors like financial services, supply chain management, and identity verification, promoting greater security and efficiency. Blockchain is a system for recording information in a way that makes it difficult or impossible to change, cheat, or hack. Imagine it like a digital ledger or notebook that is shared among a network of computers. Each piece of information, or "block," is added to the ledger in a line or "chain." When a block of information is added, it's verified by everyone on the network. Once they agree it's legitimate, it is added to the chain of previous blocks, and once a block is added, it can't be changed without altering all the blocks after it. This security feature helps prevent tampering. The entire blockchain is visible to everyone within the network, making everything transparent and accountable. This technology is the backbone of cryptocurrencies like Bitcoin, but it's also used in various other ways, such as securing medical records, voting systems, etc.

Environmental and Energy Innovations: With climate change and sustainability becoming increasingly urgent, innovations in clean energy and sustainable technologies are becoming increasingly crucial. Developments in renewable energy sources, carbon capture and storage, and sustainable urban planning are critical for addressing environmental challenges.

Space Exploration and Colonization: The enduring interest in space exploration and the potential colonization of other planets, such as Mars, poses unique technological, ethical, and social challenges. These endeavors could redefine what it means to be human and expand the boundaries of human civilization to other planets.

As these technologies develop and intersect, they promise to alter the fabric of human existence fundamentally. This could profoundly change societal structures, economies, and individual lives. However, the ethical, philosophical, and logistical challenges accompanying these transformations will require novel governance approaches, policy frameworks, and a redefinition of human identity. Just as previous revolutions have reshaped humanity, the paths we choose in response to these new technologies will significantly influence the future trajectory of our civilization.

I envision a future where advanced technological gadgets are central to managing our daily lives. This technological proliferation promises to streamline mundane tasks and enhance our efficiency. Still, it also presents significant challenges regarding humans' role in a world increasingly dominated by machines.

As automation and artificial intelligence continue to evolve, many traditional roles and jobs that humans currently hold are likely to be taken over by machines. This shift could lead to a fundamental rethinking of work, identity, and economic systems. The question then becomes: What unique contributions can humans make in a machine-driven world?

The philosophical debate, once considered largely theoretical, concerning whether to throw a man off a bridge to stop a runaway train and save lives—illustrative of the classic trolley problem—has gained practical significance in the age of artificial intelligence, particularly in the context of autonomous vehicles. This ethical dilemma explores the decision-making process when faced with a moral choice that involves sacrificing one life to save many others.

As autonomous or self-driving cars become more integrated into daily transportation, these AI-driven systems are programmed to make split-second decisions that could potentially involve life-and-death scenarios. The trolley problem has thus transitioned from a purely philosophical exercise to a tangible challenge for engineers and programmers of autonomous vehicle technology.

When an autonomous vehicle encounters an imminent crash, the AI must decide in an instant whom to protect—whether to swerve to avoid hitting pedestrians at the risk of endangering the passengers inside the vehicle or to protect the occupants at all costs. These decisions involve complex ethical considerations that AI systems must be equipped to handle.

Programmers are tasked with creating algorithms that can navigate these ethical dilemmas, which involves technical expertise and a deep understanding of ethical values and societal norms. This has sparked a broader discussion about the moral frameworks that should guide AI development and the extent to which these machines can make ethical decisions.

Moreover, it raises significant questions about accountability and responsibility. In situations where an autonomous vehicle makes a decision that results in harm, determining who—or what—is responsible becomes complicated. Is it the manufacturer, the software developer, the car's owner, or the AI itself?

As this technology evolves, ongoing discussions and regulations must evolve alongside it to address these ethical challenges. By doing so, society can ensure that autonomous cars, airplanes, container ships, and drones operate with high efficiency and safety and in a manner that aligns with the ethical expectations and values of the community.

One crucial aspect that machines have yet to replicate fully is emotional intelligence—the ability to recognize, understand, and manage not only one's own emotions but also to empathize with the emotions of others. Despite advancements in AI, including developing algorithms that can interpret human facial expressions and voice intonations, the nuanced understanding of human emotions and the complex responses that these emotions elicit are deeply rooted in biological and psychological processes that machines cannot completely emulate.

Emotional intelligence involves more than just recognizing emotional cues; it also encompasses navigating social situations, managing interpersonal relationships judiciously and empathetically, and making decisions that achieve positive emotional outcomes for all involved. These skills are becoming increasingly crucial as technology reshapes our interactions and social paradigms.

Cultivating emotional intelligence will be vital as we grapple with a technology-driven society's ethical and practical implications. It will distinguish human capabilities in the workplace and beyond. Roles that require empathy, compassion, and emotional nuance—such as counseling, teaching, healthcare, and leadership—

will likely become even more critical, highlighting the enduring value of human touch in our interactions.

Humans evolved from Homo habilis to Homo erectus to Homo sapiens, adapting on a macro level to ensure survival and on a micro level to thrive in diverse environments and climates. Homo habilis, known for its use of stone tools, marked the beginning of this evolutionary journey approximately 2.4 million years ago. Homo erectus, emerging around 1.9 million years ago, exhibited more advanced tool use and control of fire, which were crucial for survival. Finally, Homo sapiens, appearing about 300,000 years ago, developed complex language, art, and technology, allowing for sophisticated adaptation and cultural development.

Throughout each evolutionary stage, humans lost certain physical attributes that once helped us survive, such as speed, muscle strength, and acute senses. However, they gained other traits that were advantageous for adaptation.

In cold environments like the Arctic, humans have evolved shorter, stockier bodies to conserve heat and narrower nasal passages to warm the air before it reaches the lungs. Conversely, in hot, arid environments such as deserts, people tend to be taller and leaner to dissipate heat more effectively, with darker skin to protect against UV (ultraviolet) radiation.

Humans living at high altitudes have developed increased

lung capacity and hemoglobin levels to improve oxygen uptake, which is essential for surviving in low-oxygen environments. Darker skin protects against UV radiation in tropical rainforests, and efficient sweating mechanisms help cool the body. Coastal populations often have increased fat storage for insulation and buoyancy, aiding in swimming and heat retention.

These adaptations have enabled Homo sapiens to thrive in a variety of environments worldwide, showcasing the remarkable flexibility and resilience of our species in the face of diverse ecological challenges.

Fast-forward to the present day. We rely heavily on our cognitive abilities and intelligence to survive and preserve the human species. As we continue to depend on technology in the future, there is a concern about whether we might lose some of our cognitive abilities and intelligence.

If this were to happen, it could fundamentally alter human capabilities and how we interact with the world. The potential implications for humanity include a greater reliance on artificial intelligence and machines to perform tasks requiring cognitive functions, possibly leading to a significant shift in human work, learning, and problem-solving. This reliance could result in the atrophy of specific mental skills, similar to how physical skills have diminished due to modern conveniences.

However, it's important to note that human cognition has always been dynamic, shaped by the tools and technologies we use. The future may see humans augmenting their cognitive abilities with technology rather than losing them, integrating advancements like brain-computer interfaces to enhance our natural capabilities. The key will be finding a balance that leverages technology to improve human life while maintaining and developing our innate cognitive abilities.

Historically, humans have continuously adapted to new tools and environments. For example, the development of written language thousands of years ago was initially seen as a threat to memory and oral traditions. Yet, it led to unprecedented advancements in knowledge sharing and cultural development. Similarly, calculators and computers have taken over many manual calculation tasks, allowing humans to focus on more complex problem-solving and creative endeavors.

In the future, technologies such as artificial intelligence, machine learning, and brain-computer interfaces could augment human intelligence. These technologies could assist in quickly processing vast amounts of information, providing new insights, and enabling more effective decision-making. Far from diminishing our cognitive abilities, they could open new horizons for human thought and creativity.

While there are concerns about the potential impact of technology on human cognition, history shows that humans have always adapted to new tools and technologies in ways that ultimately enhance our capabilities. The challenge will be to ensure that we use technology to complement and expand our cognitive abilities rather than replace them, thereby preserving the essence of what makes us uniquely human.

Renowned historian and author Yuval Noah Harari offers a thought-provoking quote: "History began when humans invented gods, and it will end when humans become gods." This statement encapsulates some of the core themes explored in his works, particularly in "Sapiens: A Brief History of Humankind" and "Homo Deus: A Brief History of Tomorrow." In "Sapiens," Harari discusses the development of human societies and how mythmaking, including the creation of gods and religions, has been central to societal organization and cohesion. "Homo Deus," on the other hand, looks forward to a future where humans might transcend their biological limitations, essentially gaining 'god-like' powers through advancements in technology such as genetic engineering and artificial intelligence. Harari's quote reflects his exploration of these vast epochs in human development—from our humble beginnings, dominated by myths and gods, to a future potentially controlled by extraordinary human advancements.

Harari extends this discussion into the future with his

speculation about humans becoming like gods, not through divine connection but through technological advancements. He posits a scenario where future technologies could allow humans to enhance their physical and cognitive abilities, create life, manipulate fundamental biological processes, and even potentially conquer death, achieving what might be seen as God-like powers. This raises ethical and philosophical questions about the nature of power and the role of human beings within the universe. What happens when humans attain such powers? Will the same patterns of consolidation of power, as seen with those who claimed to be divine representatives, emerge again?

This potential future invites reflection on past lessons, the dangers of unchecked power, and the ethical implications of profound technological capabilities. As we advance, these developments' philosophical and ethical considerations are critical. Harari's exploration serves as both a caution and a call to think critically about our paths as we approach these god-like thresholds.

As we continue integrating more sophisticated technologies into every aspect of our lives and possibly embed them to overcome our biological limitations, focusing on and developing emotional intelligence will ensure that humans retain an irreplaceable role in a world increasingly influenced by machines. This balance between leveraging technological advancements and enhancing our unique human qualities will be vital in navigating the future effectively.

Emotional intelligence, emphasizing empathy, interpersonal skills, and self-awareness, complements the capabilities of machines and reinforces our social and collaborative strengths.

In a technologically advanced world, human qualities such as creativity, ethical judgment, and emotional understanding will become even more valuable. These attributes enable us to connect deeply with others, foster innovation, and make decisions that consider the broader impact on society. By prioritizing the development of these skills, we ensure that technology serves humanity rather than diminishes it.

Historically, adopting new technologies has often led to significant societal changes, but humans have consistently adapted by evolving our skills and finding new ways to thrive. A concerted effort to cultivate emotional intelligence alongside technical proficiency will be essential as we move forward. This approach will help us maintain our unique human identity and use technology to create a more inclusive, empathetic, and resilient society.

Our ability to harmonize technological innovations with the intrinsic human qualities that machines cannot replicate will define the future. By fostering emotional intelligence and embracing technological advancements, we can navigate the complexities of the modern world and build a future where technology enhances, rather than replaces, the human experience.

Venture Forth: Navigating the Path to Entrepreneurial Success

"Do not be embarrassed by your failures, learn from them and start again." - Richard Branson

When my wife, Samira, and I started our business, the entrepreneurial landscape was distinctly different from what it is today before the advent of the digital revolution. Starting a business typically required substantial capital investment, access to physical premises, and significant overhead costs, making it a risky venture. Consequently, only a tiny fraction of those who ventured into business ownership succeeded. The barriers to entry were high, scaling a business was even more challenging, and the resource requirements often excluded many potential entrepreneurs.

The digital revolution has radically transformed the landscape of entrepreneurship, particularly in the business-to-consumer (B2C) market, by dramatically lowering the costs and barriers to starting a business. Today, the rise of the internet and digital technologies means that anyone with a compelling idea can launch a startup with far less initial capital than was traditionally required. This democratization of entrepreneurial opportunities has ignited a surge in startups, especially within the tech sector, reshaping the face of modern business.

One of the most significant changes brought about by the digital era is the access to global markets from the outset. Digital platforms, with their worldwide reach, allow startups to tap into international markets almost immediately. This global audience enables businesses to scale rapidly, achieving growth that was much more challenging in the pre-digital era. For instance, social media platforms like Facebook and Instagram have become pivotal for even small businesses, allowing them to reach a global audience through targeted advertising and interact directly with customers worldwide.

Moreover, the shift to digital has reduced the need for heavy capital investments traditionally associated with starting a business. Online operations can now bypass the requirement for physical stores, large staff, and other costly resources. E-commerce platforms like Shopify or Amazon and cloud services provided by companies like Amazon Web Services and Google Cloud allow new businesses to minimize upfront investments in physical infrastructure and IT departments, making the entrepreneurial path more accessible than ever.

Innovation in monetization strategies has also been a hallmark of the digital era. New revenue models, including subscription services, freemium plans, in-app purchases, and targeted advertising, have provided businesses with various ways to generate income. These models allow companies to tailor their revenue strategies precisely to their products and market demographics. For example, many mobile apps and games are free but generate revenue through advertisements, in-app purchases, or even user data sales. This approach significantly lowers user acquisition barriers and increases market penetration.

Another advantage of digital businesses is their ability to rapidly iterate on their products based on real-time user feedback. Online analytics tools provide insights into user behavior and preferences, enabling companies to make quick adjustments that enhance service quality and user satisfaction. This level of agility was less feasible in a pre-digital business environment, where feedback loops were slower and adjusting strategies was both time-consuming and costly.

Finally, the digital revolution has expanded access to funding. Crowdfunding platforms like Kickstarter allow entrepreneurs to raise capital directly from future customers, bypassing traditional funding routes. Additionally, venture capital and angel investing growth has substantially boosted promising startups, particularly those operating in the technology and digital sectors, fueling further innovation and growth.

The digital revolution has transformed how businesses operate and redefine what is possible, offering unprecedented opportunities for innovation, growth, and global expansion in the entrepreneurial landscape.

While the digital revolution has lowered entry barriers and expanded the tools available to entrepreneurs, success is not guaranteed. The same factors that lower barriers for one entrepreneur do so for others, increasing competition dramatically. Moreover, while it is easier to start a business, the challenges of scaling, maintaining customer engagement, and achieving profitability remain significant.

The digital revolution has redefined what it means to be an entrepreneur. It has opened new paths to success and provided tools that allow individuals to turn innovative ideas into viable businesses more readily than ever before. However, greater competition and new challenges come with increased opportunities, underscoring the need for strategic planning, innovation, and effective execution in the quest for business success.

Our foundational principles were distinctive and deeply personal when we embarked on our entrepreneurial journey. The core of our ethos was a genuine passion that drove our efforts—this wasn't merely about pursuing profit; it was about creating something precious that resonated deeply with us, our customers, and the broader community.

We envisioned a business that stood for more than just financial success. We aimed to forge meaningful connections through our products and services that directly addressed our customers' needs and aspirations. This approach often prioritizes customer satisfaction and long-term engagement over immediate financial gains. It required a deep understanding of who our customers were, their value, and how our offerings could significantly meet those needs.

Sustainability was another guiding principle, and we viewed it in a holistic sense—not just in environmental terms but as sustaining a business model that fostered steady growth and made a positive community impact. We implemented socially responsible and environmentally friendly practices, ensuring that our operations contributed positively to society. Our goal was to build a business that could prosper without compromising the ethical standards we had set.

While financial stability is undoubtedly necessary for any business, accumulating wealth was never our sole focus. We gauged our success by financial metrics, the fulfillment we derived from our work, and its impact on the community. This perspective shifted our focus from merely achieving short-term financial results to realizing longer-term personal and social benefits.

Staying true to our principles and core values was crucial, especially when faced with challenges. In the business world, it's easy to be swayed toward decisions that may conflict with your initial values under pressure. From the outset, we committed to maintaining the integrity of our vision, convinced that adherence to our foundational values would navigate us through turbulent times and lead to authentic and enduring success.

These principles shaped our business from the ground up, providing a strong foundation aligned with our ideals and aspirations. This alignment guided our business decisions and helped us build a fulfilling venture on a deeper personal level.

Starting and running a business on these principles demands more than mere enthusiasm; it requires a commitment to creating something that enriches lives and adheres to a broader purpose. It's about forging a path that others can follow, inspiring your team, and positively impacting your community. This approach nurtures a loyal customer base and builds a resilient business capable of withstanding the ebbs and flows of economic cycles.

Even in the face of adversity, commitment to perseverance catalyzes surmounting obstacles and realizing one's aspirations. Moreover, we understood that setbacks are not terminal endpoints but integral components of the broader trajectory toward achievement. Thus, we approached setbacks as opportunities for growth, demonstrating the adaptability and tenacity necessary to forge ahead on their entrepreneurial odyssey.

Recognizing that you cannot do everything yourself is a

crucial insight into the business world. This realization often marks a significant turning point for many entrepreneurs and business leaders, leading to more sustainable and effective management practices.

Individuals can only be an expert in some aspects of a business. Specialization allows people to focus on what they do best, enhancing both efficiency and quality of work. By delegating tasks to individuals with the appropriate skills and knowledge, a business can leverage a wider range of expertise than anyone could offer.

Time is finite, and effective time management is critical in business. Understanding that you can't do everything helps prioritize tasks that align with your strengths and significantly impact your business goals. Delegating or outsourcing other tasks frees up time to focus on strategic planning and growth initiatives.

Acknowledging that you can't handle every task alone underscores the importance of building a solid team. A well-rounded team brings diverse perspectives and skills to the table, which can lead to more innovative solutions and better decision-making. Effective team building involves hiring competent people, trusting them to manage their responsibilities, and fostering a collaborative work environment.

A business that depends too heavily on the capabilities of a single person is difficult to scale. For a company to grow, it must have systems and a team that can function efficiently, even as demands increase. Recognizing your limitations is the first step toward creating these scalable business processes.

Trying to manage every aspect of a business can lead to burnout. This affects personal health and well-being and can compromise decision-making abilities and leadership effectiveness. By delegating tasks and allowing others to share the workload, leaders can maintain a better work-life balance, which is crucial for long-term success.

A good leader recognizes when to step back and let others lead. This helps develop the next generation of leaders within your organization and strengthens the team by showing trust in other members' abilities.

Team chemistry plays a vital role in the success of any company, just as harmony is essential in an orchestra. A cohesive team that works well together is the foundation of a thriving organization. Leadership often requires tough decisions to maintain this harmony and promote collective success. Prioritizing team dynamics fosters a collaborative work environment where individuals can flourish and achieve their full potential.

When you free yourself from the day-to-day tasks by delegating them, you allow more room for creativity and strategic thinking. Innovation often comes from exploring new ideas and approaches, which can be stifled when overwhelmed with operational tasks.

In essence, understanding that you cannot do everything is not just about acknowledging your limitations—it's about making strategic decisions that enable your business to thrive. It involves building a supportive infrastructure that leverages collective strengths to achieve common goals. This approach enhances business efficiency and contributes to a more adaptive, innovative, and resilient organization.

In business, various analogies from sports, military, and other fields illustrate effective team management. Sports analogies compare managers to coaches who develop skills and foster teamwork, while military analogies emphasize clear hierarchical structures and mission-focused strategies. Orchestra analogies highlight the importance of synchronizing diverse talents to create harmony, and ecosystem analogies stress interdependence and adaptability within a team. These comparisons provide valuable insights into leadership, communication, and fostering a cohesive and resilient team environment.

We selected the orchestra analogy to build and manage our team at NNOVIM. This approach encapsulates the idea that a successful team, like a well-conducted orchestra, requires a blend of diverse talents, precise coordination, and a shared vision to create beautiful music—or achieve outstanding results in the case of a business.

In an orchestra, each musician plays a specific instrument. Similarly, in a business team, individuals bring different skills, experiences, and perspectives. The diversity in skill sets—from creative thinking and technical expertise to strategic planning and customer engagement—is crucial. Each team member, like each musician, has a vital role in the overall performance. Recognizing and valuing these different roles ensures that the team can function harmoniously and effectively.

Just as an orchestra requires precise timing and coordination to produce a cohesive sound, a business team needs to synchronize its efforts to achieve common goals, this involves clear communication, mutual respect, and regular collaboration. Like skilled conductors, effective leaders guide their teams through complex projects and initiatives, ensuring everyone is aligned and moving together in rhythm.

The role of the conductor in an orchestra is crucial—they not only keep time but also interpret the music score and lead the emotional expression of the piece. In business, leaders must provide clear direction and inspire their team, setting the tone and pace of work. They must be adept at reading the "room," understanding the dynamics at play, and adjusting their leadership style to bring out the best in each team member.

An orchestra spends countless hours practicing, refining their skills individually and as a group. Similarly, a successful business team must commit to continuous improvement, lesson learning, and adaptation. This could involve training, professional development, and feedback mechanisms that encourage growth and address areas needing improvement.

Ultimately, the goal of an orchestra is to perform in harmony, creating a unified sound greater than the sum of its parts. For a business team, the equivalent is creating a cohesive unit where the collective effort leads to success. This requires a culture of support and teamwork, where successes are celebrated together, and challenges are met with a collective resolve.

Just as musicians adjust their performance based on the conductor's cues and audience reactions, effective teams are responsive to feedback from leadership and clients. This adaptability allows the team to continuously refine its strategies and outputs, ensuring it remains relevant and competitive.

Embracing the orchestra analogy can profoundly impact how a team operates and performs. It underscores the importance of each member's contribution, the necessity of skilled leadership, and the beauty of creating something remarkable through collaboration. This approach enhances the team's effectiveness and creates a more fulfilling and dynamic work environment.

Optimism is a cornerstone trait for entrepreneurs, imbuing them with the requisite mindset and resilience to confront the myriad challenges in their journey. Recognizing that failures are inevitable waypoints along the path to success, entrepreneurs must possess the fortitude to press forward, undeterred by setbacks. Genuine self-belief and a steadfast

As a business grows and progresses through different stages, its challenges and competitive landscape inevitably evolve. Transitioning successfully from one stage to a higher one often requires significant changes in strategy, operations, and management practices.

As a business scales, the leader's role must also evolve. Initially, business leaders might be deeply involved in day-to-day operations, but as the organization grows, they should shift toward strategic oversight and long-term planning. This transition often involves delegating routine tasks to trusted team members and developing a leadership style that guides and inspires others rather than managing every detail.

Small businesses often operate with a flat organizational structure. However, as a company grows, this can lead to inefficiencies and bottlenecks. A more hierarchical or sophisticated matrix structure can help maintain oversight and specialization levels. This also involves defining clear roles and responsibilities, which can enhance efficiency and accountability.

With growth comes increased complexity in operations, customer management, and strategic decisions. Businesses may need to invest in more advanced management information systems, enterprise resource planning (ERP) systems, or customer relationship management (CRM) tools to handle this complexity effectively. These systems can streamline operations and provide the analytical insights to make informed decisions.

Preserving a cohesive company culture becomes challenging as more employees join and the business environment becomes more diverse. Leaders must actively cultivate a culture that supports the company's core values and mission while embracing flexibility and innovation. This might involve regular training sessions, team-building activities, and open communication channels to ensure the growing team remains aligned and motivated.

As the scale of operations increases, managing finances becomes more complex and critical. It may be necessary to bring in specialized financial expertise in the form of a CFO or a dedicated finance team who can oversee budgeting, forecasting, and investment strategies to ensure the company's financial health and compliance with regulatory requirements.

As businesses grow, they often encounter new competitors

and increased customer expectations. It's crucial to evaluate and adapt market positioning continually. This might involve diversifying product lines, enhancing service offerings, or rebranding to ensure the company remains competitive and relevant in a changing market.

Adaptability stands as a foundation trait in the realm of entrepreneurship. The dynamic evolution of a business demands leaders who are flexible and open to change. In the nascent stages of a venture, business owners often wear multiple hats, juggling diverse responsibilities. However, delegating tasks and entrusting others with significant responsibilities becomes imperative as the company scales and expands. This transition can prove challenging, particularly for entrepreneurs deeply entrenched in their company's operations, as it necessitates relinquishing control. Nevertheless, embracing this change is paramount for sustaining the growth and prosperity of the business and fostering an environment conducive to innovation and progress. It's a journey marked by apprehension and excitement as leaders navigate new roles and relationships while striving to maintain the entrepreneurial spirit that ignited their venture's inception.

To reach and sustain higher levels of success, businesses must commit to ongoing innovation and improvement. This involves staying abreast of industry trends, customer needs, and technological advancements. Encouraging a culture of innovation can involve setting up dedicated R&D teams, collaborating with external partners, or investing in startup ventures.

Potential risks magnify with growth, making effective risk management strategies crucial. These include identifying potential risks early, developing contingency plans, and ensuring adequate insurance coverage and compliance protocols.

Transitioning to a higher level of operation is a significant challenge for any business, requiring adjustments in almost every aspect of its operations. Leaders must be proactive, adaptable, and forward-thinking to manage this growth effectively and ensure the company survives and thrives in its new environment.

As a business evolves, so too must the leadership. Understanding and anticipating these shifts in roles—from doing and directing to empowering, envisioning, and enabling—can make the difference between a company that merely survives and one that thrives. Each phase demands different skills and focuses, and a successful leader can adapt to these demands while keeping the team engaged and aligned with the company's goals.

The evolution of a leader's role is crucial as a business progresses through its various phases. Effective leadership is dynamic; it adapts to the shifting needs of the organization and the team. As a company grows and changes, so must the way a leader approaches their role.

In the early stages of a startup, a leader often acts as a primary operator, handling day-to-day tasks and hands-on problem-solving. As the business stabilizes and grows, the leader must transition into a more visionary role, setting long-term goals and defining the company's strategic direction. This shift is crucial for ensuring the organization stays energized, innovates, and adapts to market changes.

Initially, leaders may find themselves involved in every minor decision and process. However, as the organization grows, effective delegation becomes critical. This involves identifying the right people for the right tasks and trusting them to take responsibility. Delegation helps manage increased workloads. It empowers other team members, fostering a sense of ownership and accountability within the team.

As a business matures, a leader should increasingly focus on coaching and developing employees. This shift is about moving beyond mere delegation to actively mentoring and supporting team members to reach their full potential. Coaching helps build a more capable and motivated team, which is essential for the ongoing health and growth of the business.

Effective communication is vital at all stages, but as a company grows, the complexity and importance of clear communication also increase. Leaders must ensure that communication channels are open and effective, vertically within and horizontally across different departments. The goal is to keep everyone aligned with the company's mission, values, and strategic objectives.

In the early days, a company's culture might naturally evolve from the small team's dynamic. As the organization grows, intentionally cultivating and maintaining a positive and cohesive culture becomes a key role for leaders. This includes reinforcing core values, recognizing and celebrating achievements, and ensuring that the workplace environment supports all employees' well-being and professional growth.

As companies grow, the stakes in decision-making get higher. Leaders must enhance their strategic thinking and risk management skills, analyze more complex scenarios, and make decisions that will affect the company in the long term. This involves assessing current resources and capabilities and forecasting future trends and potential disruptions.

Finally, leaders must become adept at managing change. Whether implementing new technologies, restructuring the organization, or entering new markets, leaders must guide their teams through transitions smoothly and effectively. This requires a combination of emotional intelligence, strategic foresight, and change management skills.

One of the most demanding challenges business owners face is balancing the dual responsibilities of safeguarding the company's future while also considering the well-being of employees. These decisions often involve significant ethical and practical considerations and can profoundly impact the organization's culture and morale.

As a leader, balancing personal interests with those of the employees involves understanding that the business's health ultimately supports everyone dependent on it. Sometimes, this might mean prioritizing the company's long-term sustainability over short-term benefits to employees or even the owner. This could involve strategic pivots that may not be popular but are necessary, like restructuring or cost-cutting, which could include layoffs.

Transparency in decision-making builds trust, even when the decisions are tough. When employees understand the reasons behind significant changes or difficult choices, they are more likely to accept them, even if they are adversely affected. This means openly communicating about the state of the business, the challenges it faces, and the rationale behind the decisions being made.

Ethical considerations should guide business decisions, especially when compromises are needed for the company's greater good. This includes ensuring fairness and avoiding discrimination against any group of employees. For instance, if layoffs are necessary, offering severance packages, support in finding new employment, or retraining opportunities can help mitigate the impact on affected employees. Additionally, providing outplacement services and creating a supportive environment for remaining and departing employees is crucial. Recognizing and addressing the emotional impact of these decisions on all employees is also important for maintaining a positive and ethical workplace.

In times of change, prioritizing ongoing communication is vital. Keeping dialogue open helps to alleviate uncertainties and rumors that can damage morale. Regular updates and allowing space for employees to voice their concerns or ask questions can help maintain a sense of inclusivity and respect.

When making tough decisions, it's essential to focus on the long-term health and growth of the business. While immediate effects might be painful, decisions that ensure the company's survival are often in the best interest of the broader base of employees, stakeholders, and the community in the long run.

Sometimes, the business owner must make personal sacrifices to benefit the company and its employees. This might include cutting their salary to reduce operating costs or investing personal funds to keep the company afloat. Such actions can demonstrate commitment to the company and its employees, strengthening trust and loyalty.

Ultimately, how these difficult decisions are handled can define a company's culture. Leaders who act with integrity, transparency, and genuine concern for their employees can maintain a positive work environment, even during challenging times. This approach not only helps in navigating immediate crises but also in building a resilient and committed workforce.

Starting a business soon after college can indeed lead to great success, as seen in high-profile cases in the tech industry and other sectors. However, these stories often represent exceptions rather than the norm. Experience in established organizations before venturing into entrepreneurship provides vital advantages crucial for long-term success and stability.

Working for an established company allows aspiring entrepreneurs to learn about organizational structures and business operations practically. This experience is invaluable for understanding how different departments interact, the flow of communication, and the roles of various team members. Observing these dynamics firsthand can teach crucial lessons about effective management and leadership.

Effectively dealing with employees, customers, and business partners is a skill honed through experience. Working in an established environment exposes you to different personalities and situations, helping you develop interpersonal skills and customer service expertise. These skills are essential for running their own business, impacting team management, customer satisfaction, and, ultimately, business success.

When you start your own business, you are responsible for your livelihood and your employees. Experience in other organizations can teach you about the weight of this responsibility. You learn the importance of making decisions that ensure the security and welfare of your team and understanding the broader impact of your business decisions.

Businesses inevitably face periods of growth and struggle. Working in an existing business exposes you to its cyclical nature and teaches resilience. You learn strategies for handling economic downturns, managing stress, and navigating challenges, which are critical skills for any business owner.

Experience helps one understand risk assessment and management, a key business aspect. Learning to identify, evaluate, and mitigate risks in an established business setting can prevent costly mistakes and ensure more stable decision-making when starting a venture.

Working in a specific industry before starting a business allows you to build a professional network of mentors, peers, and potential future partners or customers. These relationships can be crucial for support and opportunities as you start and grow your business.

Being involved in a business gives you insight into financial management, budgeting, and the economic aspects of running a company. This includes understanding cash flow, profit margins, and financial forecasting, which are all crucial for the success of a new business.

While starting a business without professional experience can be successful, the skills, knowledge, and resilience developed through working in other environments are invaluable. They prepare one for the practical aspects of running a business and help build the emotional and strategic acumen needed to navigate the complexities of entrepreneurship.

Embarking on the journey of starting your own business is both challenging and rewarding. Entrepreneurship demands resilience, creativity, and an unwavering commitment to your vision. As you navigate the complexities of building a business, remember that the foundation of success lies in thorough planning, adaptability, and the ability to learn from failures. Surround yourself with a supportive network, leverage diverse talents, and maintain a clear focus on your goals. By embracing the entrepreneurial spirit, you create opportunities for yourself and contribute to innovation and economic growth. The path of entrepreneurship is not always easy, but perseverance and passion can lead to extraordinary achievements and a fulfilling career.

Faith: Exploring the Realm of Religion

"My faith is brightest in the midst of impenetrable darkness." -
Mahatma Gandhi

Faith and religion, while often discussed interchangeably, actually denote two distinct concepts. Faith refers to a personal, internal conviction or trust in something or someone, which doesn't necessarily require empirical evidence to exist. This belief can be spiritual but isn't limited to religious contexts—it might also encompass faith in an idea, a person, or a principle. On the other hand, religion is a structured, organized system characterized by rituals, practices, and established beliefs about spirituality or divinity. Typically involving communal activities and institutions like churches, religion provides a formal framework through which individuals can express and nurture their faith. Thus, faith is primarily a personal spiritual journey, whereas religion offers a communal and systematic way to engage with and express that spiritual journey.

I've always valued the role of early religious education in imparting ethical and moral teachings to children. Introducing them to such concepts through religion can deeply influence their character and values, equipping them with a strong moral compass for navigating the complexities of life. It helps children develop respect for diverse beliefs and cultures and lays a solid ethical foundation, fostering integrity and empathy as they grow.

While I deeply appreciate the timeless wisdom found in the teachings of various religious traditions, my personal beliefs about these teachings diverge somewhat from traditional religious doctrines. I do not view myself as religious in the conventional sense. Instead, I see the prophets celebrated in different faiths not as divinely appointed messengers but as extraordinarily insightful individuals who emerged in response to the needs and challenges of their times. This perspective shapes my understanding of morality and ethics, highlighting the importance of human insight and historical context in forming our moral ideals. Through religion, we can access and cultivate a profound sense of faith that enriches our moral and ethical understanding.

I perceive prophets as deeply understanding human nature and societal dynamics. They recognized the challenges and issues of their times and sought to address them by establishing ethical and moral guidelines. In doing so, they often invoked the concept of a higher power or a superpower. This strategy was employed to ensure that their teachings gained traction and adherence. By presenting their ideas as divinely inspired or mandated, these influential figures were able to impart a sense of greater authority and urgency to their messages.

Their teachings, often encapsulated in religious texts and doctrines, were spiritual guidelines and a form of early social governance. They laid down principles that aimed to enhance individual well-being and, concurrently, the collective good of society. In essence, these prophets can be seen as early social reformers who used the concept of a higher power to bring about positive change and instill a sense of communal ethics and morality.

This viewpoint acknowledges the significant impact these figures have had on human history and culture, but it frames their contributions more as a result of human insight and wisdom rather than divine intervention. It values the essence of their teachings while attributing their origins to human ingenuity and understanding of societal needs.

In my life's journey, I have encountered people deeply devoted to various faiths. This has granted me a rare insight into the varied spectrum of religion, the divine messages they carry, and the profound impact these beliefs can have on an individual's life.

As I navigated these diverse religious landscapes, I learned more about the doctrines and rituals and how people integrate these teachings into everyday existence. I've met individuals who seamlessly weave the basic principles of their faith into every aspect of their daily lives, demonstrating how religion can guide everything from simple daily choices to major life decisions.

On the other hand, I have also encountered those at the more extreme end of the spectrum. These encounters have been eye-opening, showing me the lengths some will go in the name of faith. I've seen acts committed under the banner of religion that range from the incredibly selfless to the incomprehensibly extreme.

These experiences have taught me that faith, in its many forms, is a powerful force in human life. It can shape personal and communal identities and profoundly influence actions and worldviews. I researched, studied, and tried to gain an understanding of the vast, complex world of religious belief and the myriad ways it manifests in the lives of the faithful.

In the complex history of human society, individuals often find a sense of belonging and identity through their affiliations with various communities and groups. These associations, whether based on interest, geography, or ideology, are vital in shaping an individual's self-concept and worldview. However, an unintended consequence of these affiliations is the tendency to differentiate and, at times, elevate one's group above others. This demarcation becomes a tool for both identity formation and social division.

Particularly striking is the role of religion in this context. Religion, inherently deep-rooted and often intertwined with one's core identity and worldview, does not merely connect like-minded individuals; it also has the potential to create profound rifts.

Adherents of a specific faith may firmly believe in the exclusivity and supremacy of their religious truths.

While providing a strong sense of community and purpose within the group, this belief can marginalize those outside it. Other religions, with their differing doctrines and practices, may not only be viewed with skepticism but sometimes with outright hostility. This dynamic is starkly evident when individuals of one faith label those of another as 'infidels,' a term laden with connotations of not just religious otherness but also moral and existential wrongness.

This phenomenon underscores a paradox inherent in human associations: the same structures that foster community, support, and shared understanding can also lead to segregation and conflict. The intersection of religion with social and cultural identities compounds this effect, as religious beliefs often command a profound commitment that transcends other affiliations. The challenge, therefore, lies in balancing the human need for belonging and identity with the cultivation of a broader perspective that embraces diversity and fosters mutual understanding and respect."

In interpreting this, it's essential to recognize that while associations like religion can be sources of comfort and community, they also have the power to create barriers between people. The key is not to eliminate these differences but to learn how to appreciate and understand them, fostering a world where diverse beliefs coexist harmoniously.

Throughout history, religious authorities have often positioned themselves as intermediaries between the divine and the people. This was notably prevalent in medieval Christianity in Europe, and it's similarly observable in a few Muslim-majority countries today. These religious leaders have wielded significant influence, often proclaiming themselves as representatives of God.

While I have always respected individual faith and each person's unique relationship with their religion and God, my observations and experiences have led me to view the intersection of religion and governance with a critical eye. Particularly concerning is when those in power exploit religious beliefs to exercise control over society. Such manipulation distorts the essence of the faith and can lead to the erosion of individual freedoms and rights.

A glaring example of this can be seen in the actions of certain religious governments, such as the one in Iran following the 1979 revolution. There, the Islamic government agents, under the guise of spiritual authority, have been accused of committing acts that starkly contradict the core principles of the religions they claim to uphold. From corruption, rape, theft, and to acts of violence and murder, these actions stand in direct opposition to the teachings of peace, justice, and morality found in nearly all religious doctrines.

This misuse of religious influence for political or personal gain betrays their followers' trust in these leaders. It underscores the need for vigilance in distinguishing genuine spiritual leadership from those who would use religion as a tool for their ends. Such reflections have only deepened my belief in the importance of separating personal faith from political authority and ensuring that religion remains a source of comfort and guidance, not a tool for manipulation and control.

Delving into the origins of various world religions reveals a fascinating story of beliefs, many tracing their earliest influences to ancient religions in regions like Persia. These ancient belief systems laid the foundational concepts, rituals, and myths that were later adapted or absorbed into significant world religions. Modern religions' spiritual, mythological, and ethical ideas are deeply rooted in these ancient traditions, illustrating a profound interconnectedness across the ages. In ancient times, stories, myths, and moral lessons were passed down orally from generation to generation, evolving with each retelling and influenced by diverse cultures and experiences. Different messengers of God, prophets, and spiritual leaders adopted and adapted these stories, incorporating them into their teachings. This process suggests that many religious messages may not have been direct communications from a deity but rather a collection of ancient wisdom and cultural heritage.

Zoroastrianism, one of the world's earliest monotheistic faiths, emerged from ancient Persia and significantly shaped the religious landscape of subsequent monotheistic religions. Its doctrines of dualism, embodying the perpetual struggle between good and evil, as well as ideas about a final judgment and a messianic savior, have left a lasting imprint on Judaism, Christianity, and Islam. The notion of an apocalyptic end of the world also traces its roots back to this ancient faith.

The Ancient Egyptian religion, with its intricate polytheistic belief system and emphasis on the afterlife, has also influenced modern religious thought. The Egyptians' practice of judging the deceased by weighing their heart against the feather of Ma'at (symbolizing truth) parallels similar concepts in Christianity and Islam.

In the cradle of civilization, the Sumerians introduced narratives that have permeated through time, such as the flood story in the Epic of Gilgamesh, which echoes the biblical and Quranic flood stories, showcasing the cross-cultural transmission of religious tales.

Hinduism, one of the oldest practiced religions today, has profoundly influenced not only its direct offshoots like Buddhism and Jainism but also broader religious thoughts with its concepts of reincarnation and karma. The philosophical depths of Hindu scriptures and rituals continue to resonate across various religions and philosophies.

The mythologies of ancient Greece and Rome have permeated the fabric of early Christian thought, art, and culture. Incorporating pagan rituals and festivals into Christian traditions underscores the fluidity with which religious practices can evolve and adapt.

The ancient Chinese religious philosophies of Taoism and Confucianism emphasize harmony with nature and rigorous social ethics. These principles have transcended regional boundaries, influencing various East Asian religions, including adapting Buddhist practices across China, Korea, and Japan.

Indigenous religions from around the world, with their profound reverence for nature and ancestral worship, continue to influence modern religious and ecological spiritual movements, highlighting the universal themes of connectivity and respect for the earth.

Ancient religions have contributed to later religions' spiritual and moral framework and demonstrated religious development's dynamic, syncretic nature throughout human history. This legacy of synthesis and adaptation highlights the enduring quest for understanding and interpreting the human experience through the lens of the sacred.

CURRENTS OF BEING

I will explore Zoroastrianism in more detail, an ancient religion that originated in Persia and stands out for its foundational role in developing subsequent religious traditions. By examining Zoroastrianism, we can understand its significant impact on the ethical, spiritual, and philosophical concepts of many of today's monotheistic religions. As one of the world's oldest monotheistic religions, Zoroastrianism offers a profound yet straightforward guide to ethical living. Its foundational principles have subtly influenced many subsequent religions and philosophies, leaving an enduring legacy that continues to shape our spiritual and moral framework.

Zoroastrianism is centered around three simple but powerful tenets: Good Thoughts, Good Words, and Good Deeds. These principles form the core of its ethical system, and it emphasizes the importance of performing them. This triad is more than just moral guidance; it is a holistic approach to life that encourages individuals to strive for righteousness in every aspect of their existence.

The emphasis on Good Thoughts underlines the importance of intentions and attitudes, advocating for a mindset that fosters positivity, compassion, and understanding. Good Words highlights the power of words and their impact on the world. Zoroastrianism teaches that words can heal or harm and thus should be used wisely and kindly. Finally, Good Deeds is about actions, the tangible expressions of one's thoughts and words, urging adherents to engage in actions that positively contribute to society and the world. Their other principles include:

Zoroastrianism is known for its concept of dualism, which posits the existence of two fundamental and opposing forces: Ahura Mazda (the Wise Lord) representing truth, order, and light, and Angra Mainyu (the Destructive Spirit) embodying deceit, chaos, and darkness. Followers are encouraged to align themselves with Ahura Mazda in the perpetual struggle against Angra Mainyu.

Ahura Mazda is the supreme god in Zoroastrianism. The name "Ahura Mazda" translates to "Wise Lord" or "Lord of Wisdom" in Avestan, the sacred language of the Zoroastrian texts.

Ahura Mazda is characterized as the creator of the universe, the source of all light and wisdom, and the embodiment of good. He is opposed by Angra Mainyu (also known as Ahriman), the destructive spirit and the embodiment of evil. This dualistic conflict between good (represented by Ahura Mazda) and evil (represented by Angra Mainyu) is central to Zoroastrian cosmology and theology.

Today, Ahura Mazda remains a central figure in Zoroastrian worship, which continues to be practiced by Zoroastrians around the world, particularly in Iran and India (where the followers are known as Parsis). The ethical and moral principles championed by Ahura Mazda in Zoroastrian texts continue to resonate with modern adherents, emphasizing truth, purity, and righteousness as the ways to combat the forces of chaos and evil.

Understanding Ahura Mazda offers insights into the philosophical and theological underpinnings of Zoroastrianism. It highlights themes of moral choice and the importance of good thoughts, good words, and good deeds—principles that have universal appeal and were the foundation of many religions to come thereafter.

When these principles are studied, for example, in the context of Zoroastrianism, it becomes apparent how they have echoed down the ages, influencing other religious doctrines, secular philosophies, and ethical frameworks. This ancient religion's emphasis on moral rectitude, personal responsibility, and the interconnectedness of thought, speech, and action has been a guiding light, directly or indirectly shaping various cultures and societies' moral and ethical underpinnings.

Understanding the roots of such religious philosophies provides a deeper appreciation for the commonalities in moral and ethical teachings across different faiths. It highlights the shared human endeavor to seek meaning, purpose, and guidelines for righteous living, transcending geographical, cultural, and temporal boundaries. This exploration into the origins and principles of ancient religions like Zoroastrianism enriches our understanding of the past and offers timeless wisdom that remains relevant in guiding contemporary society.

The Faravahar, a prominent symbol of Zoroastrianism and Persian heritage, represents the divine spirit of Ahura Mazda. It features a winged disc with a human figure at its center, embodying fundamental Zoroastrian principles such as good thoughts, words, and deeds. The symbol's elements include a central human figure symbolizing the soul, a ring denoting eternity, wings representing ethical living, and streamers highlighting the duality of existence. Recently, many young Iranians have worn the Faravahar as a powerful statement of their cultural roots and a subtle yet touching expression of their discontent with the Islamic government ruling Iran. This act of wearing the Faravahar underscores a connection to their ancient heritage and a desire for an identity distinct from the current political regime.

Religions offer individuals a profound sense of faith and a comprehensive moral framework. They provide guidelines for ethical behavior, promote community cohesion, and offer solace and hope in times of hardship. For many, religious teachings are deeply respected and serve as a guiding force for making the right decisions in life.

However, when a single religion is imposed on diverse groups or when religious authority is misused to govern, it can lead to significant backlash and the erosion of human rights. This is evident not only in some Muslim-majority countries but also in other contexts. In Iran, Saudi Arabia, and Afghanistan, religious doctrines have been used to justify laws that limit women's freedoms, such as restrictions on dress codes, mobility, and participation in public life. Similarly, in parts of India, the enforcement of Hindu nationalist policies has led to the marginalization of religious minorities, infringing on their rights and freedoms.

In addition, historical examples such as the Catholic Church's influence during the Spanish Inquisition demonstrate how religious authority can be misused to suppress dissent and enforce conformity, often through severe and inhumane measures. The World Economic Forum's Global Gender Gap Report highlights that countries with stringent religious laws often have wider gender gaps compared to more secular nations.

These examples illustrate that the imposition of religious doctrines, regardless of the specific faith, can lead to significant human rights issues, especially when such doctrines are not adapted to respect contemporary values of equality and freedom.

Moreover, the use of religion to justify violence against non-believers or those of different faiths is fundamentally wrong and contradicts the core teachings of many major religions. For instance, Christianity preaches love and compassion towards all individuals, as reflected in Jesus' commandment to "love your neighbor as yourself" (Mark 12:31). Similarly, Islam, at its core, emphasizes peace, with the Quran stating, "There shall be no compulsion in [acceptance of] the religion" (Quran 2:256), highlighting the importance of freedom of belief.

Using religion as a justification for murder or violence not only distorts the true message of these faiths but also contributes to cycles of hatred and retribution. Such actions violate the fundamental human rights to life and freedom of belief, leading to widespread suffering and division. Religious leaders and followers must reject these misinterpretations and work towards fostering an environment of mutual respect and understanding.

The historical context of many religious doctrines also poses challenges in modern societies. These guidelines, often formulated centuries ago, may not align with contemporary values and human rights standards. The Universal Declaration of Human Rights, adopted in 1948, emphasizes the need for universal and inalienable freedoms and rights, including gender equality, which sometimes conflicts with traditional religious practices.

While religion can be a powerful force for personal and communal good, promoting ethical behavior and offering spiritual comfort, its role in governance and societal norms must be balanced with modern human rights principles. Ensuring that religious practices do not infringe upon the rights and freedoms of individuals, particularly in diverse and multicultural societies, is essential. The evolution of religious interpretation in harmony with contemporary values is necessary to foster a society where everyone, regardless of gender or belief, can live with dignity and freedom. This balance can be achieved through dialogue, education, and a commitment to upholding universal human rights.

Although religion can significantly promote ethical behavior and provide spiritual comfort, it must be practiced in a way that respects the rights and freedoms of all individuals. Misusing religious authority to impose doctrines or justify violence undermines the fundamental principles of most faiths and poses a significant threat to human rights and social cohesion. A balance between religious practices and contemporary human rights is essential for fostering a just and equitable society.

It is also important to recognize that many religions, despite their differences and the reluctance of some believers to accept other faiths, share common roots and often convey similar messages about our role in the world. These religions frequently emphasize principles of compassion, justice, and the importance of living ethically. By acknowledging these shared foundations, we can promote greater understanding and unity among diverse religious communities, reinforcing the idea that, at their core, many faiths strive to guide us towards a harmonious and purposeful existence.

Mindful Senses: Navigating Happiness Through Sensory Awareness

"The best way to capture moments is to pay attention. This is how we cultivate mindfulness." - Jon Kabat-Zinn

When our daily routines and activities momentarily pause, our minds often do not. Left unoccupied, our mind can quickly become our prison, entrapping us in cycles of reflection and anticipation that may lead to psychological distress. Dwelling on past events can lead to depression as we ruminate over regrets or missed opportunities. Similarly, focusing too much on the future can generate anxiety fueled by uncertainties and the fear of what might or might not happen.

In today's hyper-connected world, even our moments of rest and relaxation are frequently interrupted. If we're fortunate, we can secure a good night's sleep and perhaps a few hours of rest over the weekend—or even a week of vacation in a year or two. However, these precious periods of downtime are often punctuated by a continuous stream of social media, text messages, and emails, all accessible through our ever-present smart mobile devices. This constant connectivity means that genuinely stepping away from work and daily responsibilities can feel almost impossible.

CURRENTS OF BEING

The concept of being 'always on' can significantly damage our mental and physical health. It blurs work and personal life boundaries, leading to stress and burnout. The expectation of being perpetually reachable and responsive erodes our ability to relax and recharge fully. Even during planned vacations, essential for our well-being, many find it difficult to disconnect fully, detracting from the therapeutic benefits these breaks should provide.

In response to these challenges, it is increasingly important to establish firm boundaries with technology. Strategies such as setting specific 'off' times when devices are turned off or notifications are silenced can help. Employers can also play a role by promoting a culture that respects personal time, emphasizing that employees are only expected to respond to work communications during regular working hours if it's an emergency. Encouraging such practices enhances individual well-being and contributes to a healthier, more productive work environment.

This mental state suggests that humans may not be inherently equipped for the fast-paced, highly scheduled lifestyles that modern society has developed. Today, we interact with technology that operates at the speed of light, manage calendars blocked in tight increments, and juggle more responsibilities than perhaps ever before. This relentless pace can be overwhelming, demanding constant attention and energy, leaving little room for mental rest or reflection.

Historically, human beings lived much simpler mental lives deeply connected to nature and the rhythms of their environment. Unlike today's artificial and often frenetic schedules, this connection provided a natural cadence to daily activities. As a result, the modern lifestyle can sometimes feel at odds with our intrinsic needs for downtime, reflection, and deeper connection with our surroundings and community.

The challenge lies in finding a balance between leveraging the benefits of advanced technologies and managing the mental and physical demands they impose. We may need to cultivate practices that ground us in the present and help us manage our thoughts about the past and future. Mindfulness, meditation, and dedicated periods of disconnection from digital devices are examples of practices that can help manage the psychological impacts of modern life. By intentionally creating spaces for mental rest, we can mitigate the feeling of being prisoners of our own minds and instead use our cognitive capacities to enhance our well-being and quality of life.

Since I focused on Artificial Intelligence in my graduate study, I have been deeply interested in understanding how the brain functions and analyzes sensory information. This fascination taps into the core of cognitive neuroscience, offering endless insights into human nature and the biological underpinnings of our perceptions and experiences. Exploring the mechanisms of brain function enriches our understanding of AI and provides a profound appreciation of the complex processes that shape our interactions with the world.

The human brain, a marvel of complexity, processes sensory information in ways central to understanding our biological functioning and behavior. The latest neuroscience research reveals a fascinating interplay between our sensory organs and the brain, illuminating how we perceive the world around us.

Each of our senses—vision, hearing, touch, taste, and smell—is equipped with specialized receptors that are finely tuned to detect specific types of stimuli. For instance, photoreceptor cells in our eyes capture light and convert it into electrical signals, while mechanoreceptors in our skin are triggered by mechanical pressure or distortion. This initial stage of sensory reception involves the direct interaction of our sensory organs with the external environment, capturing the raw data of physical phenomena.

Once these receptors have detected a stimulus, they embark on the signal transduction process, translating physical inputs into electrical impulses. This conversion is crucial, transforming sensory inputs into a language the brain understands. The nature of these signals varies depending on the stimulus and the sensory system involved, setting the stage for complex neural communications.

These electrical impulses are then transmitted through neurons to specific brain regions designated for processing different types of sensory information. Visual signals are routed to the visual cortex, auditory signals to the auditory cortex, and so on. This signal transmission ensures that information reaches the appropriate neural centers for further processing.

Upon arrival in the brain, these signals undergo perception and analysis. During this phase, the brain interprets the electrical signals by integrating them with existing information and memories. This intricate integration process allows us to recognize a familiar face, understand spoken words, or instinctively pull back from a hot surface. It's where raw data becomes meaningful perception, enabling us to interpret and interact with our environment effectively.

Finally, the brain generates an appropriate response based on this complex analysis and interpretation. This could range from a simple reflex to dodge a fast-approaching object to a complex decision-making process like navigating through a crowded room. The pathway from initial stimulus to final response encapsulates numerous parts of the brain and myriad neural connections, each playing a critical role in shaping our interactions with the world.

Through this continuous flow of reception, transduction, transmission, perception, and response, our brains manage to translate the external world into experiences and actions, illustrating the profound capabilities of our neural architecture.

Books and research in neuroscience often explore these processes in greater detail, discussing how various factors such as attention, memory, and learning influence sensory processing and perception. Understanding these mechanisms helps us know how we interact with the environment and how perception and sensory processing disorders can occur, impacting overall brain function and behavior.

For example, the phenomenon where a smell or taste triggers vivid memories, often from childhood, is known as the "Proustian phenomenon" or "olfactory memory." It's fascinating how our brain and memory function together to connect sensory experiences with memories.

Consider Marcel Proust's famous example in his book "In Search of Lost Time," where the taste of a madeleine dipped in tea evokes a surge of memories from his childhood, which is a classic illustration of this process. This example has given the name to the phenomenon where seemingly forgotten memories return to the mind after encountering certain smells or tastes. The animated film Ratatouille also provides a beautiful and illustrative example of how taste can evoke deep-seated memories. In a particularly memorable scene, the food critic Anton Ego tastes the ratatouille prepared by Remy, the rat chef, and he is instantly transported back to his childhood. This dish triggers a powerful and emotional memory of being comforted by his mother in his childhood home after a bad day.

The deep connection between our senses and emotions is vividly illustrated through sensory memories tied to taste and smell, which can powerfully evoke past experiences. Such moments show how a simple, rustic dish might provoke a profound emotional response in someone accustomed to sophisticated cuisine, not just because of the flavor but also because of its association with the comfort and love of childhood.

This process starts with the olfactory pathways, unique among the senses; when we detect a smell, olfactory receptors in the nose process the odor molecules and send signals directly to the olfactory bulb at the brain's base. This bulb is closely linked to the amygdala and the hippocampus, critical areas in the brain for emotion and memory.

Because of these direct connections to the brain's emotional centers, smells can trigger emotions and memories more readily than other sensory inputs. The amygdala and hippocampus play critical roles in processing emotional responses and transforming short-term memories into long-term ones.

The initial experience of a particular smell or taste, especially during formative years, is deeply embedded in our memory, intertwined with the emotions felt, the setting, and the people involved at that time. Encountering the same sensory stimuli later in life can trigger these ingrained memories, often bringing a vivid recollection of those moments. This intricate interaction between our senses and memory underscores how deeply intertwined they are in shaping our emotional experiences.

Unlike visual or auditory information, which does not pass directly through these emotional brain centers, smell and taste are directly linked to emotional memory. This connection makes them more likely to trigger emotional memories, explaining why certain scents or flavors can evoke such strong emotional reactions and carry a profound sense of nostalgia.

This phenomenon is why, as we get older, our comfort food tends to be what we grew up with. Studies have shown that the brain regions responsible for processing smells and tastes are closely linked to the limbic system, which is involved in emotion and memory. Thus, the sensory experiences of our childhood, especially those related to food, become powerful triggers for emotional recall and comfort in adulthood. This can significantly affect our eating habits, as we may seek out familiar and comforting foods from our past to evoke feelings of safety and nostalgia, influencing our dietary choices and preferences throughout life.

Understanding these neurological processes sheds light on the fascinating ways our brains operate and underscores the deep interconnection between our senses and our emotional experiences.

This intricate relationship explains why particular smells and tastes can unleash such powerful emotional responses and why they remain nostalgically significant throughout our lives.

The decline in the acuity of human senses over the course of civilization is not just a matter of cultural change; it reflects significant shifts in our lifestyle and environment that have lessened the necessity for keen sensory perception in daily survival. To better understand how our senses have adapted and dulled compared to our ancestors or skilled professionals today, let's delve deeper into each sense with more detailed examples.

Historically, hunter-gatherers' survival relied heavily on their acute sensory awareness and keen attention to every detail of their surrounding environment. Their ability to detect subtle changes in the landscape, track animal movements, and identify edible plants was crucial for finding food and avoiding dangers. This heightened perception enabled them to adapt and thrive in diverse and often challenging ecosystems.

They needed sharp vision to identify threats from predators and spot prey from a distance. Their eyes were likely fine-tuned to detect subtle movements and slight variations in the natural environment, which provided crucial survival information. In stark contrast, modern humans spend significant time indoors, frequently engaged with screens with artificial visuals requiring minimal visual depth and range. Numerous studies have linked increased screen time to a higher prevalence of myopia (nearsightedness), suggesting that our modern lifestyle, with its lack of need for distance viewing, might be reshaping our visual capabilities. Meanwhile, professionals such as artists and designers actively train to enhance their perceptual skills, enabling them to notice and utilize subtle differences in color and form that most people overlook, applying these nuances in their creative endeavors.

In prehistoric times, the ability to discern faint sounds in the environment was critical for survival. The acute hearing allowed early humans to evade predators and hunt effectively. Today, however, most urban environments are inundated with constant background noise, which may desensitize our hearing capabilities. In contrast, musicians and audio engineers meticulously train their ears to detect fine nuances in pitch, tone, and rhythm, skills that enable them to produce and appreciate complex soundscapes. For example, a trained musician might detect a slight off-key note during a concert—a detail that would typically escape the general audience.

Similarly, our hunter-gatherer ancestors had to rely on their sense of taste to evaluate the safety and quality of foods, as certain flavors, particularly bitterness, could indicate toxicity. Modern diets, dominated by processed foods high in sugars, salts, and fats, tend to overwhelm these subtler flavors and reduce our palate's sensitivity. However, culinary professionals like chefs and sommeliers undergo extensive training to discern and appreciate the delicate balances in food and wine. These experts can often identify not just the ingredients but also the methods of preparation and, sometimes, even the region of origin, similar to how a sommelier can pinpoint the subtle notes and body of a wine that suggest its vineyard and vintage.

The sense of smell, too, was vital for early humans to track food sources and detect dangers, such as the approach of a fire or spoiling food. Today, our continuous exposure to pollutants and chemicals can impair our olfactory functions, and many of us live in sanitized environments largely devoid of natural scents. Nevertheless, professionals like perfumers and oenologists (wine experts) develop their sense of smell to extraordinary levels, enabling them to identify and create intricate scent and flavor profiles. A skilled perfumer, for example, can discern the complex layers of a fragrance, recognizing the distinct base, middle, and top notes composed of various scents.

The sense of touch, like the sense of smell, played a crucial role in early human survival. It allowed our ancestors to navigate their environments, identify objects, and detect potential threats. The tactile sense enabled early humans to recognize different textures, temperatures, and pressures, essential for finding food, crafting tools, and building shelters.

Although our lifestyles may have changed in modern times, the importance of touch remains. Continuous exposure to various environmental surfaces and materials can still influence our tactile sensitivity. Professions such as physical therapists, craftsmen, and musicians develop their sense of touch remarkably. A skilled physical therapist, for instance, can detect subtle changes in muscle tension and texture, enabling them to provide precise and effective treatments. Similarly, a craftsman can feel the finest details in their materials, ensuring the highest quality in their work.

Musicians, especially those who play string instruments or pianos, rely heavily on their sense of touch. They must develop a refined sensitivity to the pressure and movement required to produce the desired sound. This heightened tactile awareness allows them to express various emotions and nuances through their music.

While modern lifestyles may not demand the sensory acuity once essential for human survival, there is considerable value in enhancing our sensory perceptions. Reconnecting with and refining these abilities can improve our interactions with the environment and deepen our appreciation for professional crafts and the nuances of the natural world. This perspective encourages us to integrate more sensory engagement into our daily routines, potentially enriching our experiences and broadening our understanding of our surroundings.

Just as our bodies require regular exercise to remain fit and healthy, our brains need continuous stimulation to stay sharp. We often spend hours in the gym, training each muscle group meticulously, yet we tend to leave our brains to navigate the complexities of daily life without dedicated training. To foster a healthy brain, it's essential to go back and actively engage with, appreciate, and train our senses. This practice revitalizes our sensory perceptions and enhances overall cognitive function.

By engaging in activities that stimulate our senses—such as cooking, which enhances taste and smell; listening to or creating music, which refines our auditory skills; participating in visual arts, which improve our visual and spatial reasoning; or practicing yoga and meditation, which heighten our sense of touch and body awareness—we can strengthen neural pathways and enhance sensory acuity. These activities, involving complex sensory input, act as workouts for the brain, improving neural connectivity and cognitive health.

For example, cooking requires distinguishing between different flavors and aromas, which sharpens our taste and smell senses. Listening to or playing music involves recognizing pitches, rhythms, and harmonies and fine-tuning our auditory abilities. Engaging in visual arts, such as painting or sculpture, helps improve our visual perception and spatial reasoning by requiring us to interpret colors, shapes, and perspectives. Practicing yoga and meditation increases our awareness of touch and proprioception, the sense of the relative position of one's own parts of the body, by focusing on the sensations and movements of our bodies.

Similarly, regularly challenging our brains with new learning experiences, such as learning a different language, solving puzzles, and tackling complex problems, can help maintain cognitive sharpness and prevent the mental stagnation often associated with aging. Sensory stimulation is crucial in maintaining neuroplasticity, allowing the brain to continue forming and reorganizing synaptic connections in response to new learning or sensory experiences.

Incorporating regular mental exercises and sensory challenges into our lifestyle is as vital as physical fitness routines. Activities like learning a new language, practicing mindfulness, or engaging in arts and crafts stimulate the brain and enhance our overall cognitive health. This holistic approach—caring for both body and mind—is essential for living a balanced, fulfilling life and ensuring we remain vibrant, engaged, and capable throughout our lives. By nurturing our senses and cognitive abilities, we prepare our brains better to handle the challenges of both today and tomorrow.

Although the field of psychology has made tremendous strides, offering various medications and therapeutic approaches to address the challenges faced by our brains, there's still much to be said for the proactive maintenance of mental health in healthy individuals. Just as we invest time and effort in physical fitness to maintain our bodily health, nurturing and developing our mental faculties is equally important.

Working on our senses and continuously refining them, as our ancestors did, can significantly enhance our cognitive abilities and overall well-being. This approach corrects deficits and enriches our perceptual experiences and mental resilience. For instance, individuals challenged by one sense often develop heightened abilities in their other senses. Blind individuals frequently enhance their hearing, touch, and even smell abilities. This adaptive response illustrates the brain's remarkable capacity to reorganize and strengthen the remaining senses to compensate for the loss of one. This adaptation is a testament to the brain's remarkable plasticity— its ability to reorganize and adjust in response to new challenges or changes in sensory inputs.

When I first took up painting as a hobby, I was struck by how it expanded my perception of the world. Initially, I aimed to emulate those skilled painters who could discern countless shades of green within a single landscape or capture the subtle gradations of blue and the formation of clouds in the sky—nuances that typically escape the everyday observer. As I practiced, I noticed how artists interpret and recreate the world with such depth and detail; every shadow became meaningful, hinting at the direction and intensity of light and adding dimension to the scene.

This new hobby did more than teach me to paint; it fundamentally changed how I see things. Shadows were no longer just dark patches; they were vital, dynamic aspects of each view, indicating the time of day, weather conditions, and even the texture of objects. The practice of painting trained my mind to appreciate these details, enhancing not only my artistic skills but also my everyday sensory experiences. This shift in perception is a testament to the brain's adaptability and capacity for learning, demonstrating how engaging in creative activities like painting can enrich our understanding and interaction with the world.

Focusing intently on the task at hand helps us stay present and engaged in the moment. In today's era, characterized by widespread attention deficits, the rapid pace of technological innovations—such as mobile phones, text messaging, and social media—has significantly diminished our ability to concentrate. The pervasive use of smartphones and social media platforms has dramatically altered our attention spans, making it increasingly difficult to maintain sustained focus. These digital distractions constantly compete for our attention, leading to a fragmented and less productive approach to managing tasks and responsibilities.

According to a study by Microsoft, the average human attention span has decreased from 12 seconds in 2000 to just 8 seconds in 2013, a phenomenon often attributed to the digital age and the constant influx of information from electronic devices. This relentless stream of notifications, updates, and messages fragments our attention, making it challenging to focus on a single task for an extended period.

A more recent research conducted by the World Economic Forum in 2021 found that half of the surveyed UK adults felt their attention spans were shorter than they used to be, largely attributing this decline to the constant influx of information from digital devices. The average person significantly underestimated how frequently they checked their phones, guessing around 25 times a day, whereas the actual number ranged between 49 and 80 times daily.

Moreover, the format of our social media content also plays a role. Platforms like TikTok and Instagram promote short-form content, training our brains to seek quick, brief stimulation and making it harder to maintain focus on longer tasks. This trend has been particularly pronounced among younger generations, such as Gen Z, who have grown up with these technologies and show the shortest attention spans.

These findings underscore a broader concern about how modern technology is affecting our ability to focus. While long-term studies are still needed to confirm these trends definitively, the current data suggest that the digital age, with its myriad distractions, contributes to shorter attention spans and a more fragmented approach to consuming information.

Addressing this issue may involve strategies such as monitoring and reducing screen time, engaging in mindfulness practices, and encouraging activities that require sustained focus, like reading or learning a new skill. By becoming more aware of how we interact with technology, we can better manage its impact on our cognitive functions and attention spans.

Continuous exposure to digital stimuli can lead to cognitive overload, where the brain struggles to process the excessive information it receives. This overload hampers our ability to concentrate and contributes to higher stress levels. A study published in the Journal of Applied Research in Memory and Cognition found that multitasking with digital devices can increase stress and reduce productivity. Frequently checking our devices disrupts our focus and prevents us from being fully present in the moment. Research by the American Psychological Association indicates that the constant switching between tasks, known as task-switching, can reduce efficiency and impair our ability to stay engaged with a single activity. This distraction-laden environment affects our professional lives and personal interactions, as we are often more focused on our screens than the people around us.

To counteract these effects, practices such as mindfulness and attention training are increasingly recommended. Mindfulness, the practice of bringing one's attention to the present moment, has improved concentration, reduced stress, and enhanced overall well-being. A study by Harvard Medical School found that mindfulness meditation can increase the thickness of the prefrontal cortex, which is associated with attention and sensory processing.

While technological advancements have brought numerous benefits, they have also reduced our ability to focus and stay present. By acknowledging the impact of digital distractions and incorporating practices like mindfulness, we can enhance our attention span, reduce stress, and improve our overall quality of life. These measures underscore the importance of addressing the challenges posed by our digital environment and adopting strategies to improve our attention and focus.

We can counteract these effects by consciously engaging our sensory awareness and improving our attention to the present moment. This heightened awareness not only helps reduce stress but also improves overall well-being. By training ourselves to be more attentive and present, we can reclaim our focus and find greater peace in our daily lives.

During your next encounter with the sensory delights of the world, take a moment to ask yourself, "Do I truly feel, see, hear, taste, or smell?" Whether it's feeling the soft caress of a finely woven fabric, inhaling the captivating scent of an exquisite flower, gazing upon the breathtaking view of a stunning landscape, savoring the complex flavors of a meticulously prepared dish, or listening to your favorite music, take a moment to appreciate not just the joy these experiences bring but also the profound exercise they provide for your brain.

Engaging deeply with these sensory activities does more than offer mere enjoyment. It sharpens your mind, enhances your perceptual capacities, and enriches your cognitive landscape. Every color noted, every texture felt, every note heard, and every aroma inhaled contributes to this rich sensory experience. Each detailed observation or nuanced flavor is not just a momentary pleasure but an exercise in cognitive enhancement, training your brain to recognize, categorize, and remember complex patterns and sensory inputs.

These experiences, layered with emotions and cognitive engagement, become woven into the fabric of your memory, creating a vivid and enriching tapestry. Enhancing sensory perceptions is not just about enhancing one's sensory perceptions but about integrating these experiences into a broader understanding of the world, contributing to greater cognitive depth and emotional resilience.

As golfer Walter Hagen wisely advised, "You're only here for a short visit. Don't hurry, don't worry. And be sure to smell the flowers along the way." This reminds us of sensory experiences' profound impact on our lives and the importance of appreciating them. The benefits of immediate enjoyment and cognitive enrichment make each sensory interaction a valuable opportunity. Each sensory engagement becomes a bridge to a more attentive, perceptive, and deeply connected life. By actively participating in these experiences, you enhance your mental and emotional well-being, stay focused on the present, and elevate your overall happiness. Embrace the richness of your surroundings through your senses and let them guide you to a more fulfilled and joyous existence.

About The Author

Dr. Shahin Samadi holds a PhD from George Washington University and has had a distinguished career spanning both academia and industry. His professional journey includes significant contributions at NASA, where he amassed extensive experience in engineering and systems architecture. He has also held technical leadership roles at notable organizations, including CRM giant Merkle (now a part of the Dentsu Aegis Network) and the legal and business information provider Bloomberg BNA (now under Bloomberg).

Beyond his corporate accomplishments, Dr. Samadi has served as an adjunct professor at Johns Hopkins University, where he taught graduate-level courses, shaping the minds of the next generation of engineers and technology professionals. He is a prolific author of numerous technical papers that showcase his profound expertise and dedication to his field.

In 2003, Dr. Shahin Samadi co-founded and launched INNOVIM, LLC, a pioneering science and technology company. At INNOVIM, Dr. Samadi leverages his extensive expertise in computer science engineering, systems architectural design, and program management to develop high-value solutions. Under his leadership, INNOVIM has not only emerged as a formidable name in the science and technology sector but also as a trusted partner to various government agencies, including the National Aeronautics and Space Administration (NASA), the National Oceanic and Atmospheric Administration (NOAA), and the Department of Defense. The company specializes in deploying advanced technologies such as cloud computing, artificial intelligence, machine learning, and data analytics to manage and analyze large volumes of data, enhancing agency capabilities and efficiency.

Residing in Washington, D.C., with his wife, Samira, and their sons, Alexander and Sebastian, Dr. Samadi remains a beacon of innovation and inspiration in both his professional and personal life.

Made in the USA
Columbia, SC
09 August 2024

40194587R00137